DATE DUE

SE

AMERICAN
Passenger Arrival Records

American

PASSENGER ARRIVAL RECORDS

A Guide to the Records of Immigrants
Arriving at American Ports by Sail and Steam

Michael Tepper

Updated and Enlarged

GENEALOGICAL PUBLISHING Co., Inc.

Cover photograph courtesy of The Radcliffe Maritime Museum of
The Maryland Historical Society and the Baltimore City Archives

To my mother

Betty (Chodak) Tepper

CONTENTS

PREFACE

lthough it is generally considered a safe observation, we are no longer a nation of immigrants. A century ago, in the decade from 1880 to 1890, the rate of growth of the foreign-born population was nearly twice that of the native population, and by 1900, out of a population of seventy-six million, slightly more than ten million, or fourteen percent of the total, were born outside the United States; yet today there are no figures remotely comparable. Despite the recent influx of Asians and Hispanics, the overwhelming majority of the population are not only native-born but are children of at least second or third-generation Americans themselves. Nor is immigration the major concern that it was only a few short years ago when, in 1905, for instance, nearly one million immigrants arrived from Europe, or in 1907 when 1.2 million arrived. Awash with these new arrivals, the restriction of immigration became a matter of intense debate, and one law after another strove to deal with the problem until the question was temporarily settled with the creation of a quota system based on percentages of nationalities present in the U.S. at the time of the 1920 census. Today, of course, with the debate largely forgotten, European immigration is viewed unreservedly as one of the epic chapters of history, a phenomenon of mythical dimensions.

The springs of this historic movement of population are various and complex; however, it is not the purpose of this book to explore them or to analyze the popular push and pull theories of migration, except in a summary way, but rather to focus attention on the records that detail the arrival of European immigrants in America, to show

11

that there actually exists documentation on millions of those who took part in the great Atlantic migration. In essence, then, this is a guide to the records and archival resources that document the arrival of immigrants in America from the time of the earliest settlements to the passage of the Quota Acts three centuries later. As a guide, its sole aim is to explain what the records are, where the records are located, and what they contain, and it tries to cover the random, incidental records of the colonial period as well as the purposeful, systematic records of the nineteenth and early twentieth centuries.

Unlikely as it may seem, given the dubious archival practices of the past, passenger arrival records are surprisingly complete—the colonial and early federal periods excepted—and there are doubtless many people who will be astonished to learn what a vast body of recorded information exists—records that identify by name, place or country of origin, and various other particulars the vast majority of persons who made their way to this country in the most determined and sustained migration the world has ever known. To the skeptic who may doubt the actual extent of the records, the historian seeking answers to questions about the peopling of America, the family historian hoping to fill in blanks in the family tree, or to the merely curious who wish to acquaint themselves with the documents showing that we truly were a nation of immigrants, this book may prove interesting.

———————

Numerous people have contributed to this book with advice and information, and while I regret that I can't list them all, I would be remiss if I failed to mention Peter Wilson Coldham, David Dobson, and P. William Filby, as well as Cynthia Fox (National Archives), Ira A. Glazier (Center for Immigration Research), A.A.H. Knightbridge (Public Record Office, Kew), Eileen Perkins and Joe Garonzik (Genealogical Publishing Company), J. Gordon Read (Liverpool Maritime Museum), and Jürgen Sielemann (Hamburg State Archives).

AMERICAN
Passenger Arrival Records

THE COLONIAL PERIOD

IMMIGRATION RECORDS

The arrival of immigrants before the close of the eighteenth century is a potent image in American history, but it is largely undocumented. The reason for this is that throughout the long period from colonization to independence there was no proper framework for keeping immigration records: no uniform procedure for dealing with the arrival of immigrants and no coordinated immigration policy. Nor, except in Pennsylvania, was there any legal authority for collecting data or controlling the flow of immigration. The truth is that the large-scale movement of population from Europe to America was essential to the colonization process, and except for fears that unrestricted emigration might erode the labor base of the mother country or undermine the authority of the Church, there was little cause to restrain it. If not for this we might still be at a loss to understand why there wasn't a meter in place to count the arriving passengers, or a register in which to note the facts of their immigration.

As it happens, an official system of registration didn't emerge until the nineteenth century when a proposal for enumerating passengers arriving from abroad was adopted by Congress as a means of imposing controls on immigration. Prior to that time there had been various attempts by individual colonies to record the names of incoming passengers, but except in Pennsylvania in the eighteenth century such efforts were generally ineffectual. In Virginia, as early as 1632, for example, there had been an order to keep a record of the name, age, and birthplace of every passenger arriving at Point Comfort (Hampton Roads), presumably as a check on the growing number of "disorderly" persons entering the colony, but as far as we know nothing ever came of it.[1] And in Pennsylvania, a 1684 law required the registration of all new arrivals in the province, yet by the time this law was repealed in 1690 only two incomplete lists of arrivals had been compiled, one for Philadelphia and one for Bucks County.[2] In general, in the absence of a coherent program of registration at either colony or state level, immigrants disembarked at the various ports of entry "officially" unnoticed, dispersing to their destinations unchallenged save for the demand that they swear oaths of allegiance and supremacy to the English monarch (this was required during the earliest period of settlement in Virginia, for example).

Even for ships carrying the original colonists—the so-called first comers, first purchasers, first planters, etc.—there are few actual lists of passengers, certainly few that are undisputed. And of these—we will exclude the *Mayflower*—the names of passengers on the *Susan Constant,* the *Godspeed,* and the *Discovery* (Virginia), the *Ark* and the *Dove* (Maryland), the *Griffin* (New Jersey), and William Penn's *Welcome* are largely recorded—where they are recorded at all—in ancillary records and documents. (We could perhaps mention the English port books which identify some of the passengers aboard the twenty-three vessels comprising Penn's fleet of 1682, but this takes us into the realm of emigration records, and we would be getting ahead of ourselves.) Immigration didn't take place in an administrative vacuum, however, so it is not surprising that a small number of passenger arrival records came into being on their own account or emerged, uncertainly, from the first tentative efforts at regulation, much like the Philadelphia and Bucks County lists mentioned above. Among the earliest of such records are two passenger lists which are recorded in the minutes of the Council and General Court of Virginia. The lists of passengers aboard the *Ann* and the *Bonny Bess,* compiled sometime before 1623, are apparently all that survive in consequence of an order from the King and Privy Council directing that all newcomers to the colony subscribe to oaths of allegiance and supremacy. It is not clear from the form of the oaths (copies of which are in the Library of Congress in the miscellaneous papers of the Virginia Company) whether the colonists were to have their names "underwritten" by the colony clerk or were to sign individually, but no doubt lists of various sorts must at one time have existed.[3] Contemporary with the two Virginia lists, the 1623 "Division of Land" in Plymouth Colony, though not actually a passenger list, furnishes us with the names of some of the passengers of the *Mayflower* (1620), the *Fortune* (1621), and the *Anne* and the *Little James* (1623). Compiled by Gov. William Bradford, this extraordinary document names all heads of household residing in Plymouth in 1623 who were passengers on the aforementioned ships, plus some of the wives transported on the *Anne*. (This 1623 Division is not to be confused with the 1627 "Division of the Cattle" which was a distribution of livestock among the residents of the Colony, each of whom is named in one of the twelve lots making up the division.)[4] Slightly less obscure than these are the Boston impost records for various dates during the years 1712, 1715-16, and 1762-69. These records contain the usual details of the entrance and clearance of coastal and ocean-going vessels, much as can be found at other ports of entry, but they also list the names of incoming passengers. What is significant is that among the masses of surviving customs records, they are among the very few that document the arrival of *immigrant* passengers—not just coastwise travellers and merchants.[5] Without question, though, the best known passenger arrival records of this period are those which were in the keeping of the port of Philadelphia, arguably the most active port in colonial America and home of the largest body of passenger arrival records of either the pre- or post-Revolutionary periods.

In 1727 the Commonwealth of Pennsylvania enacted legislation designed to regulate the influx of "foreigners" into the province. An order of the Provincial Council required that lists of foreign or non-British passengers (for which read "German") be deposited with officials in Philadelphia, there being some concern that the growing number of "Palatine" arrivals posed a menace to the peace and security of the province. The lists were also supposed to include memoranda concerning the passengers' occupations, places of origin, and reasons for emigration. In addition, foreigners were to swear allegiance to the Crown, renouncing all former allegiances, and declare fidelity to the Proprietor of the province and its laws—all of which was to be subscribed and affirmed before the proper authorities. Together with the even more numerous lists of signers of the anti-Catholic oath of abjuration, required in 1729, these records were maintained throughout most of the eighteenth century, ceasing during the Revolutionary War but resuming in 1785 in a more or less unbroken sequence until

1808, when they abruptly terminate.

Housed today in the Pennsylvania State Archives in Harrisburg, the Philadelphia arrival lists represent in the aggregate the most important collection of immigration source materials of the entire eighteenth century. Comprising separate lists of the adult male passengers who subscribed to the required oaths of allegiance and abjuration, as well as a large number of endorsed "captains' lists," they identify approximately 38,000 immigrants of German and Swiss origin and provide additional information such as the names of vessels, ports of embarkation, and dates of arrival in Philadelphia. So important are these lists that several versions have appeared in print. The definitive version, far more reliable than its predecessors, is Ralph B. Strassburger and William J. Hinke's *Pennsylvania German Pioneers* (3 vols., 1934), a key work on German immigration into Pennsylvania, and one of the most important compilations of ships' passenger lists ever published.[6] Instances of this kind are rare, however, for port records prior to 1820 generally offer only limited opportunities for research.

Still, while there are few authentic records of passenger arrivals other than the Philadelphia and Boston lists, there are certain extant records that serve as plausible substitutes, records compiled at one or two removes from the port of entry which we may call "synthetic" or "inferential" records of immigration. Authoritative in their own right, a few of these synthetic records actually provide evidence linking passengers to specific vessels, though most do little more than support the inference that at some point all immigrants travelled to America under sail. For sheer historical interest the "headrights" recorded with the ancient land patents of Virginia take precedence over all other records in this genre. Headrights generally identify individuals whose passage to Virginia was paid in return for a grant of fifty acres of land for each person transported. The sponsor, or adventurer, was usually, though not always, the patentee of the land himself, and this worthy was also entitled to fifty acres for his own "adventure," i.e. for paying his own transportation. The roots of the headright system go back to the Virginia Company's "Great Charter of Privileges, Orders and Laws" of 1618 where plans were formulated to distribute land in the colony and to stimulate emigration. In the event, it turned out to be a successful method of recruitment, and as the majority of individuals who were transported in this manner bound themselves into servitude for a term of years, it proved particularly advantageous to the patentees who acquired thereby not only a fiefdom but the labor to go with it. Vast estates were on tap, and on very favorable terms. In 1653, for example, Col. William Clayborne patented 5,000 acres on the north side of the York River for the transportation of 100 persons, eighty of whom are named in the patent; five years later Thomas Wilkinson patented 6,000 acres above the head of the Potomac Creek for the transportation of 120 persons; while in 1666 Capt. Joseph Bridger and William Burgh between them patented 7,800 acres in Isle of Wight County for the transportation of 156 persons—all, save seventeen Negroes, named in the patent. "It is not to be assumed," writes Virginia historian Robert Armistead Stewart in the introduction to *Cavaliers and Pioneers* (1934), "that the claim for land in consequence of a person transported was made immediately after the arrival of the 'headright' in the Colony. . . . The headrights may have arrived in the Colony long before the patentee had entered claim for land thereby due. Nor is it to be assumed," he cautions, "that the headright is necessarily an immigrant. Even men of prominence in the Colony, through a voyage or repeated voyages to England and return, appear as 'headrights' of friends or relatives, who acquitted the cost of the passage in order to obtain the consequent land."[7] (A word or two more about these records in a moment.)

In Pennsylvania an analogous group of records evolved from that province's system of contract servitude, the means by which thousands of immigrants worked off their passage and afterwards received land, clothes, tools, and even money. From the point of view of the servant, Pennsylvania's system of contract servitude was a considerable improvement on the headright system, for under Penn's laws the servant was entitled to fifty acres of land "on easy terms" at the conclusion of his service. Indentured servants, or bond servants, commonly entered into an agreement before sailing to work a fixed term of years in return for their passage and any benefits that might accrue to them during the term of their service; others, anxious to emigrate but without prior contract, agreed with shipmasters or their agents to sell themselves and their services on arrival, thus redeeming the cost of their transportation by means of a contract negotiated at the point of entry. The redemption method of immigration flourished in Pennsylvania, and though not exclusive to it, was popular among the impecunious Irish and Germans, the latter lured into it by the blandishments of the notorious commission agents known as Newlanders. Despite legislation which had been enacted to protect servants from the most flagrant ill-usage by their masters, and which required "redemptioners" and their purchasers to register before legally appointed officials, comparatively few records of their "binding out" survive. However, from records formerly in the office of the mayor of Philadelphia there is a wealth of data on individuals who were bound out as servants and apprentices during the years 1745-46 and 1771-73, primarily Ulstermen who emigrated following the collapse of the linen industry, and German redemptioners who since the early eighteenth century had redeemed the cost of their passage by selling themselves and their families into service.[8]

Slightly less common are the synthetic records of immigration found among the records of the early churches. These take the form of sponsorships and admissions—letters of introduction, so to speak, from a congregation in the old country to a congregation in the new, affirming that a particular individual is a member in good standing and wishes to establish himself in the Faith in his new home. In the Protestant Episcopal Church these are called *letters of transfer,* in the Congregationalist Church *dismissions;* chief among these records, however, are the *certificates of removal* of the Society of Friends (Quakers), found amongst the meticulous Quaker "meeting" records. Quakers were required to produce a certificate of removal when they moved from one monthly meeting to another, and these documents, which were sometimes read into the minutes of the monthly sessions, often reveal former places of residence, names of family members, and approximate dates of departure and arrival, and are a first-rate if not first-hand record of immigration.[9] (The registers of families of the early Lutheran Church as well as the Reformed Church, though in no way comparable to Quaker certificates of removal, often yield similar data, and are likewise a formidable if unexpected repository of immigration materials.)

Scores of other inferential records are available to the researcher. There are in fact myriads of colonial records which identify persons of foreign origin and attest at least to a presumption of immigration— letters of denization and naturalization, for example, which entitled foreign-born Protestants to the rights of natural-born British subjects; muster rolls and militia lists, in particular the invaluable "size" rolls which identify soldiers' physical characteristics and places of origin;

even colony order books and council minutes. In minutes of the provincial secretary of New Netherland, for instance, we get a glimpse of the first buyers and sellers of real property in the colony, in books of land papers, the first patentees of land, and in registers of the provincial secretary, a sight of the first litigants in equity cases.[10]

Less circumstantial but still accounted miscellaneous are letters requesting permission to immigrate, petitions for sponsorship, and most intriguing of all, public declarations of arrival. Under this last head we include newspaper testimonials (in which passengers publicly thanked the captain and crew for a safe voyage), announcements of new arrivals who were to be "sold" at auction, and ads placed by recent arrivals trying to locate friends and relatives.[11] Not to be overlooked are diaries, journals, and narratives chronicling the immigration experience (remember Bradford's *Of Plimouth Plantation* and its account of the *Mayflower,* and John Winthrop's almost equally famous *Journal,* which identifies some of the main actors in the Great Migration of 1630). Still other evidence of immigration can be found in the extant records of the chartered trading companies such as the Virginia Company and the Dutch West India Company, and in lists of freemen, poll lists, and administrative day books and letter books.

To illustrate the point consider for a moment the immigration records of Virginia and Maryland. The primary records of immigration to Virginia in the seventeenth century are found in a series of land patent books housed in the Virginia State Library in Richmond. These records are one of the glories of the Commonwealth because they provide a continuous record of land granted to adventurers and planters from overseas. No comparable group of records answers so well as immigration records. Nevermind that they aren't passenger lists or ships' manifests; what is important is that they contain the names of the earliest patentees of land in Virginia and the names of the thousands of individuals they brought over as headrights—until the headright system fell into disuse at the beginning of the eighteenth century. With the possible exception of Maryland land records, the Virginia patents and headrights have no equal among synthetic immigration records of the period, despite the fact that they consist only of names and contain virtually no other detail that would link the immigrant to a ship, a date of arrival, or a place of origin. (Abstracts of practically all patents and grants recorded from 1623 to 1732 have been published in the delightfully-named *Cavaliers and Pioneers*. Compiled by Nell Marion Nugent, formerly custodian of the Virginia Land Archives, the abstracts cover all patents and grants except (from 1690) those located in the Northern Neck Proprietary.)[12]

For the colony of Maryland a similar body of records is just as effectively exploited for evidence of immigration—a series of original land patent volumes on file at the State Archives in Annapolis. These particular patents contain the names of all those who came and demanded land under the conditions of plantation obtaining in the Province of Maryland between 1633 and 1680. Since land was given free on demand, it can be assumed that the names of most of the immigrants arriving in Maryland in the first fifty years are to be found here, which is fortunate for Maryland because no list of passengers or ships has survived. As is the case with the Virginia patents, there is a published tool which provides access to the records—an index to immigrants compiled by Gust Skordas entitled *The Early Settlers of Maryland* (Baltimore: Genealogical Publishing Company, 1968).

Nor are the Virginia and Maryland patents the only records of immigrants taking up free land in the colonies. Under the Bounty Act passed by the General Assembly of South Carolina in 1761, for example, Protestant refugees from Europe were encouraged to settle in South Carolina on lands specifically set aside for that purpose. Provided first that they produce certificates showing that they were Protestants, they were entitled to petition the Council of the Colony of South Carolina for warrants of survey for land due to them under the very liberal terms of the Bounty. The petitions and the names of the petitioners were duly entered in the *Council Journals,* where for the period from 1763 to 1773 they comprise the chief record of immigration to South Carolina. (Janie Revill's *A Compilation of the Original Lists of Protestant Immigrants to South Carolina, 1763-1773* (1939; reprint, Baltimore: Genealogical Publishing Company, 1968), transcribed from the *Council Journals,* is a verbatim copy of the petitions recorded on behalf of these mainly German and Irish Protestants.)[13]

Although a great many synthetic immigration records originate from official sources—from records maintained by various authorities in compliance with sundry statutes, proclamations, or directives—and therefore carry an imprimatur of authority, they are not necessarily definitive, and like other records are subject to error, omission, and inconsistency. Moreover, some official records were compiled so long after an immigrant's arrival in this country that some of the information regarding his transit must be thrown in doubt. Records that come first to mind are those that derive from the various naturalization acts, with their petitions, oaths, and declarations made years after the immigrant's first sight of American shores. As types of immigration records, it might be argued, synthetic records are generally inferior to the more contemporaneous records which derive from documents developed at source—ships' logs, for instance, port books, cargo lists, account books, and formal agreements of passage—records that have a direct bearing on the actual voyage, literally placing the immigrant in the milieu of the ship. But despite the fact that synthetic records are largely circumstantial and don't actually establish the act of immigration, they do establish the fact of immigration, which answers almost as well.

EMIGRATION RECORDS

While comparatively few records of immigration other than those of a synthetic or inferential character are to be met with, there is nonetheless a wealth of emigration material available in the various countries of origin, the bulk of which naturally is in Great Britain. Much of this material is official in origin and reflects the frequently indistinguishable concerns of church and state. Beginning in 1606, for example, English law required that persons wishing to "pass beyond the seas" must obtain a license and take an oath of allegiance, while later enactments required that they take oaths of allegiance and supremacy and be examined as to their conformity to the discipline of the Church of England—this to "restrain the disorderly passing out of the kingdom" of persons whose religious or political tendencies were inimical to the interests of the Crown. In addition, from 1635 persons wishing to travel overseas had to affirm that they were "no subsidy men," that is, not subject to King Charles' controversial ship money tax, levied now not only on port towns to raise money for the construction and equipment of ships, as was customary in time of emergency, but in all communities in the counties of England and Wales. (Although subsequently declared illegal, this unauthorized tax was the source of considerable antagonism between Crown and Parliament and one of the principal causes of the English Civil War.) Before granting licenses to individuals to pass overseas—a practice that continued until 1679—customs officials had to certify that the various oaths had been taken and that the conditions touching church conformity had been met. That such regulations were generally enforced we have little reason to doubt, for scattered records attesting to certification survive, among them the register of a certain Thomas Mayhew who was appointed in 1637 to keep a record of all those persons who left England "to passe into forraigne partes," though all that remains of his register is a mere few months' jottings in 1637. Mayhew wasn't the first official to be commissioned to keep such a record, but his register is typical of the documents that have survived. (Not all those recorded as passing into foreign parts went straight to America, incidentally. Many whose consciences kept them from taking the required oaths went first to Holland, then to New England.) Easily the most important record of emigration from England in the decade prior to the Civil War, these registers of persons certified to pass beyond the seas, although complete only for the year 1635, and only for the port of London, are also the main source of information on the several thousand emigrants (estimates run as high as 25,000) who are believed to have come to New England in the Great Migration of 1630-42.

Regrettably, the authority granted the Virginia Company of London for trade and exploration in the New World did not carry with it an injunction for keeping emigration records; at any rate, few such records exist apart from the handful that identify shareholders, colony officials, or men "sent for plantation in Virginia."[14] True, a resolution of the Company in November 1622 shows that a register was to be drawn up to "consist of the name, age, country, profession, and kindred of each individual and was to state at whose charge the transportation was effected,"[15] but if such a register ever existed, it is not now extant. However, the revocation of the Company's charter, following King James' decision that Virginia should be ruled directly by the Crown rather than through the Virginia Company, occasioned an investigation of conditions in the colony itself, and this inquiry—by royal commission—resulted in the historic "Lists of the Living and Dead in Virginia" in 1624 and the "Muster of the Inhabitants of Virginia" of 1625. The "Muster," incidentally, is among the most remarkable of all early emigration records because it reveals not only the composition but something of the structure of the first permanent English-speaking colony in America. (Another list of 1625, similar in some respects to the "Muster" but far less informative, is the so-called "Extracte of all yᵉ Titles and Estates of Land."[16] Sent, or rather carried, to England by Sir Francis Wyatt, governor of Virginia, it is a register of planters and the patents issued in the four Virginia "corporations," or boroughs, of Henrico, James City, Elizabeth City, and Charles City, and may have been compiled in compliance with a provision of the "Great Charter" of 1618.)

The surviving records of licenses and examinations of persons wishing to pass beyond the seas can be found today in the Public Record Office in London, in Chancery Lane, amongst the records of the Exchequer; while the early Virginia censuses and patents are housed in the Public Record Office at Kew, just outside London, in the Colonial Office records. (The principal classes of records touching on emigration are divided almost evenly between the two facilities: in Chancery Lane are located records of the Exchequer, Privy Council, Chancery, and Treasury Solicitor; at Kew, records of the Colonial Office, Exchequer and Audit, Home Office, Board of Trade, Treasury, and Admiralty.) The importance of these records was recognized at least as early as the mid-nineteenth century, though it wasn't until 1874 that the publisher and antiquary John Camden Hotten published a transcription of every record of emigration he could find in the Public Record Office for the period from 1600 to 1700. Hotten's *Original Lists of Persons of Quality, 1600-1700* is the most famous of all published collections of ships' passenger lists and one of just a handful of books that can be accepted—as far as it goes—as authoritative. Its charming title, however, is misleading and perhaps just a touch facetious, for neither the term "Quality" nor the inclusive dates 1600-1700 is accurate. Not to belabor the point, all but a fraction of the work covers the years 1624-25, 1635, 1637-39, 1673-80, and 1685, while lists located throughout the book abound with the names of vagrants, stolen children, paupers, political rebels, and even "maidens pressed" (ostensibly into service or matrimony). Nevertheless, the *Hotten List,* as it is generally called, is justly renowned, and it has only now, after more than a century as the undisputed authority in its field, been superseded by Peter W. Coldham's *The Complete Book of Emigrants,* 4 vols. (Baltimore: Genealogical Publishing Co., 1987-93). The first two volumes of Mr. Coldham's work, covering the years 1607-1660 and 1661-1699 respectively, are a reworking of the Chancery records and records of the Exchequer already examined by Hotten; but to Hotten's basic list, which he has skillfully revised and augmented, Coldham has added the fascinating records of vagrants, waifs, and prostitutes who were taken from the Bridewell in London and transported to the colonies. (The Bridewell had been founded for the care of vagrant and orphaned children but by this time had evolved into a correctional institution.) He has also added a new and much improved transcription of the records—not actually in Hotten—of "servants sent to foreign plantations" from Bristol, 1654-86 (from a register kept by order of the Bristol Common Council as a check against abuses in the indenture system). And he has included a variety of other records that were not available to Hotten, whose research was conducted principally among the records of the old State Paper Office, the forerunner of the Public Record Office.

The final volumes of the Coldham opus, extending the period of coverage from 1700 to 1776 and bringing the story of English emigration in the colonial period to an abrupt if uneventful close, demonstrate convincingly that emigration in the eighteenth century was less a movement of population groups than a sporadic migration of individuals— servants, apprentices, laborers, rogues, and felons, to name the principal types. Hence the records drawn on, in addition to the usual range of documentary sources, consist of (1) plantation indentures and apprenticeship bindings; (2) port books (i.e. registers maintained at English and Welsh ports recording the names of merchants and shippers and the amount of duty extracted upon goods shipped to the colonies); and (3) orders for the pardon and transportation of condemned felons, issued in Latin and inscribed in a series of Patent Rolls until 1719. But increasingly—bar the last three years of the period (1773-76)—port books identifying shippers and their merchandise do duty as the principal (and largely conjectural) source of emigration data, and we look wistfully for a body of passenger lists of the kind that were probably stored in the London Custom House before their destruction in the disastrous fire of 1814. Still, in these final volumes we have the clearest picture of emigration from England that can be fleshed out from existing records. Indeed the four volumes together are remarkable in that they contain virtually every reference to English emigrants of the colonial period that can be found in England. They are as "complete" as the records allow, and while they identify only about 100,000 emigrants and passengers altogether, admittedly only a fraction of the total number that emigrated, they nonetheless embody all the information that could realistically be extracted from surviving sources in English archives.

The climate of conspiracy and insurrection prevailing in England in the seventeenth century, fuelled by church-state factionalism, by a mistrust of the monarchy and its predilection for Roman Catholicism, and by recurring fears of the exiled House of Stuart, gave rise to the creation of an increasingly esoteric body of emigration records. There is ample evidence, for example, that from the establishment of the Commonwealth under Cromwell in 1649 to the Jacobite risings of 1715 and 1745 the colonies were used as a dumping ground for enemies of the state. Indeed, fragmentary records of the forcible transportation of both political and military prisoners in the form of release and consignment documents are to be met with in the Public Record Office in London and the Scottish Record Office in Edinburgh (a few have also been noted in the Edinburgh City Archives). Records exist, for example, of Scots soldiers shipped to New England after the Battle of Dunbar (1650); of rebels who in 1685 joined the Duke of Monmouth in his attempt to overthrow James II and were subsequently banished to the West Indies; of Scottish Covenanters who that same year refused the oath of allegiance to the monarch and were transported to the plantations, many of them to New Jersey; and of Scots soldiers and Stuart sympathizers sent into exile after the sieges of Preston (1715) and Carlisle (1745).[17]

Long before Cromwell's time, however, it had been the policy of the government to transport certain classes of convicted felons to the colonies. As early as 1606, a year before the founding of Jamestown, the Plantation of Virginia had been recommended to the Privy Council as "a place where idle vagrants might be sent" (Coldham, *Complete Book of Emigrants, 1607-1660,* p. 1). The concept was further refined in 1611 when Governor Dale of Virginia proposed that the King "banish hither all offenders condemned to die out of common gaoles."[18] So attractive did this idea of ridding the country of undesirables prove, in fact, that between 1615 and the beginning of the Revolutionary War as many as 50,000 men, women, and children were forcibly transported from Great Britain to the American colonies, by far the largest number ending up as plantation servants in the tobacco-growing colonies of Virginia and Maryland. It may be unpalatable to some, but the fact is that recruitment for service in the tobacco colonies was achieved in large measure through the emptying of English jails. As a separate category of emigrants these transportees are the most numerous and the most thoroughly documented of all the emigrant groups prior to the nineteenth century, suggesting that to a considerable extent the southern colonies were settled by the dispossessed and the lawless.

As a rule, transportees were placed upon ships and sent to the tobacco colonies where they were sold to the highest bidder for a period of servitude lasting from seven to fourteen years, with the threat of dire penalties should they return to England before their term was out. The arrangement was a happy one for England, and continued right up to the Revolution, leaving in its wake a vast trove of documents bearing witness to the practice of enforced transportation— records of the Assize Courts and Courts of Quarter Session, Patent Rolls, Treasury papers, prison records, transportation bonds, and landing certificates. These records are widely scattered and somewhat hard to find, even in the Public Record Office, and would otherwise defy access except that the English scholar Peter W. Coldham has compiled a complete list of all those persons recorded as having been sentenced or reprieved for transportation to the American colonies between 1614 and 1775. Utilizing every available source, Coldham's *Complete Book of Emigrants in Bondage, 1614-1775* is by any standard of measurement the largest collection of names of colonial emigrants ever published in a single volume. It is thanks to his efforts that we have not only a definitive list of these transported felons but the largest and most discrete collection of colonial emigration records ever published.[19]

Very much in the mold of the Coldham work, because it treats another group of involuntary emigrants, is David Dobson's *Directory of Scots Banished to the American Plantations, 1650-1775* (Baltimore: Genealogical Publishing Company, 1983). Based on records of the Privy Council of Scotland, the High Court of Justiciary, Treasury and State papers, and Tolbooth, or prison, records, most of which are located in the Scottish Record Office, it identifies several thousand

Scots who were banished to the American colonies for political, religious, or criminal offenses. It names, for example, some of the Scots soldiers who were taken prisoner during the English Civil War and exiled to New England, Virginia, and the West Indies; it singles out the records of about 1,700 Scots who were expelled as enemies of the state during the Covenanter risings of the late seventeenth century, and it lists the names of men, women, as well as children who were banished to the colonies as a result of the Jacobite rebellions of 1715 and 1745. While it is a directory only of involuntary Scottish emigrants, it is nonetheless a significant research tool, for there are almost no other records in existence which establish a link between the early Scottish emigrant and his homeland. Although a much smaller work than Coldham's *Complete Book of Emigrants in Bondage,* its achievement in underscoring the role of enforced transportation in the peopling of the American colonies is considerable.

Smaller still is the recently published *Emigrants from Ireland to America, 1735-1743* (Baltimore: Genealogical Publishing Company, 1992), transcribed by Frances McDonnell from the pages of the obscure *Journal of the House of Commons of the Kingdom of Ireland* for 1796. Published originally in the *Journal* as a report of a special committee of the Irish House of Commons which had been appointed in 1743 to investigate abuses of the system of enforced transportation that had occurred during the previous seven years, this modest list of 2,000 transportees is the only known equivalent of English or Scottish transportation records—essentially a county-by-county list of convicted felons and vagabonds and an account of the money raised at courts of assizes and quarter sessions for their transportation. The report is doubly significant because in the 300-year history of emigration from Ireland to America there are few periods as destitute of emigration data as the mid-eighteenth century. A researcher could turn over an entire library of documents and books before finding anything of use on the subject, for the fact is that apart from documents relating to the Scotch-Irish of Ulster there are precious few records in Ireland of the thousands of men and women who emigrated in the eighteenth century. As a rule, if anything at all can be learned of these emigrants it is from records of arrival rather than departure, and they are few enough in the period concerned. Even so, from internal references in the committee's report it is clear that records of enforced transportation were maintained by county Crown offices and by county sub-sheriffs and mayors' clerks and may yet prove accessible.

In addition to the records of oaths and examinations, censuses and musters, and the historically significant records of enforced transportation and exile, there are a number of records in the Public Record Office in London that shed light on the emigration of "foreigners" to the American plantations. There are, for example, lists of Palatines who were dispatched to New York in 1710 as part of a scheme to promote the manufacture of naval stores and to strengthen the western frontier (located, variously, in Treasury Board papers, State papers, and Colonial Office records); and scattered references to some of the early settlers of Georgia who sailed from Europe under the patronage of the Earl of Egmont and General Oglethorpe (among records of the Trustees for Establishing the Colony of Georgia in America, Colonial Office records, though a more substantial list can be found in the Egmont manuscripts at the University of Georgia). There are scattered lists of French Huguenots such as the Petit-Guérard party which embarked for South Carolina in 1679 to investigate the possibilities of manufacturing silk, oil, and wine in that colony (Admiralty Secretariat papers); and there is a class of records pertaining to the naturalization, after 1740, of foreign-born Protestants in the Carolinas, Virginia, Maryland, Pennsylvania, New York, and the West Indies (Colonial Office records).[20]

Also among the holdings of the Public Record Office are the well-thumbed records of the Prerogative Court of Canterbury, which handled matters of probate affecting the personal estates of English subjects dying overseas, and records of the High Court of Admiralty, the English court that had jurisdiction over almost all civil and criminal cases affecting trade and merchandise at sea.[21] In addition, there are the various port books kept by customs officials which list vessels, dutiable goods, destinations, and names of shippers and shipping agents. The port books name only those persons who shipped merchandise for sale (personal items were not subject to duty), but this would include the many emigrants who took with them small quantities of goods for barter or sale on arrival at their destination. Among the best known are those for London, Liverpool, and Bristol which provide evidence of the emigration of some of the "first purchasers" and adventurers who arrived in the Delaware River aboard Penn's twenty-three ships in 1682.[22] There are also Audit Office records that bear on emigration, and papers of the Treasury, among which, in four large volumes, is a minute account of every person who left England and Scotland during the years 1773-76, at the height of a resurgence in emigration following the French and Indian War of 1754-63.[23] There are, besides, remnants of Customs House papers—port books and other fragments—and records overlooked by Hotten in his *Original Lists of Persons of Quality*—nearly two-thirds of the important Barbados census of 1679/80, for example, half of the island's parish registers, and all its militia rolls and lists of landholders.[24]

Finally, although not in the Public Record Office but in guildhall records and in records belonging to the corporations of such cities as London, Bristol, and Liverpool, there are registers of servants and apprentices bound out for service in the colonies. Indentured servitude played a key role in the peopling of the colonies and lasted as a method of emigration until the outbreak of the Revolutionary War. It has been estimated, for instance, that between one-half and two-thirds of all persons who went to the colonies south of New England were servants. Records of indentures, or contracts which bound the servant to give, usually, four years' service to the person buying the indenture, survive in the shape both of original indenture forms and registers. The Bristol registers of servants "sent to foreign plantations," the largest body of indenture records known, identify approximately 10,000 servants who were dispatched to the colonies between 1654 and 1686.[25] As a nearly continuous record of emigration from a single port they are without equal, having been compiled at a time when Bristol enjoyed a monopoly of the trade with Virginia and the West Indies. Trafficking in indentured servants had emerged beforehand as a profitable business, and registers like those kept by order of the Bristol Common Council were meant to discourage "spiriting"— the infamous practice of coercing or duping innocent youths into servitude—and to protect legitimate emigration agents from unwarranted charges of kidnapping. Nevertheless, since indentured servants formed probably the largest pool of labor in colonial America, the surviving records must represent only a small fraction of the estimated 300,000 to 400,000 persons who chose indentured servitude as a method of emigration.

British archives, of course, aren't the only repositories of emigration records. In Germany and Switzerland, in municipal, canton, and state archives, there exist numerous records of manumission from serfdom and certificates permitting emigration (which when not unlawful was severely restricted); and in the well-kept Lutheran parish registers there are records pertaining to the emigration of entire families, sometimes even communities, which often indicate causes, circumstances, and dates of emigration and allow for comparison with the corresponding records of arrival in Strassburger and Hinke's *Pennsylvania German Pioneers*. There are shipping contracts, passports, censuses of emigrants (Canton of Zurich, 1734-44, for example), and lists of religious sectarians and paupers who were assisted in their departure by local authorities. There are, as well, extensive community and church records, especially in the old Palatinate and Württemberg, and copious administrative records, those of Bern and Basel, for instance, providing the names of thousands of emigrants, among them some of the original members of Cristoph von Graffenried's colony at New Bern in North Carolina and some of the principals in the settlement of Purysburg in South Carolina a few years later.[26]

Strangely, the most extensive body of German emigration materials of the period is found not in German archives but in the Public Record Office at Kew, namely, papers relating to the distressed Palatine emigrants recently arrived in London from Rotterdam. Fleeing from a country laid waste by a brutal winter (the winter of 1708-09 was said to be the worst in over a century), and resolved at the same time to escape the thraldom of petty princes and to distance themselves from the havoc wrought by the French armies in the Rhine and Neckar valleys, refugees from the Palatinate, along with others from Baden, Bavaria, Alsace, and Württemberg, poured into England via Rotterdam with the intention of settling ultimately in Pennsylvania or the Carolinas. Initially, the English government encouraged them in their designs, but before long a number of dissenting voices were raised—first on behalf of English settlers already in the colonies, then by churchmen anxious about the number of Catholics among the Palatines, and then by various political factions in this most factional of ages—the result being that by the summer of 1709 thousands of destitute Palatines were stranded in tented encampments around London waiting leave to proceed on their journey to the New World.

The situation was a desperate one for the hapless Palatines, who in the meanwhile were accused of being a burden on the government, of reducing the scale of wages, and of taking jobs away from the English. Where previously there had been harmony between the communities, tension now rose, and camps and settlements around London were attacked and a number of Palatines set upon and killed. In near panic, the government persuaded several thousand Protestants to settle in Ireland, but after some disappointment a third or more of this contingent abandoned their new homes and returned to London. Then, in January 1710, some 600 Palatines were permitted to leave for the Carolinas. (The remnants of this party, incidentally, along with a larger company of Swiss immigrants, helped to found New Bern.) The final breakthrough came in April when, at the government's direction, 3,000 Palatines sailed for the Hudson River Valley of New York to join the small party under the leadership of Rev. Joshua Kocherthal which had been permitted to leave in 1708.

To redeem the cost of their passage, and in consideration of the large sums advanced by the government towards maintaining them, the Palatines agreed to settle on lands assigned to them in New York and to employ their powers in the production and manufacture of naval stores (tar, pitch, timber, rosin, hemp, etc.). This proved to be a happy expedient, for at one stroke it solved the Palatine problem, provided the means of ending England's dependence on foreign suppliers for naval stores, and secured the manpower sought by the colony of New York for the defense of its western frontiers against the French and the Indians. (Ultimately, only the first of these aims was fully realized.) Thus was this largest single contingent of emigrants in colonial times diverted from Pennsylvania and the Carolinas to New York.

The whole remarkable episode is brilliantly recounted by Walter Allen Knittle in *Early Eighteenth Century Palatine Emigration* (1937), to which the reader is referred not only for the historical narrative but for the appendices, which comprise lists of Palatine emigrants from Treasury Board papers and Board of Trade correspondence (Colonial Office) now in the Public Record Office at Kew. (See note 20.)

By contrast, French records of emigration are disappointingly sparse. Investigations by various writers have suggested that the reason for this is that the French viewed themselves more as entrepreneurs than colonists. Furthermore, as there was some concern that the stations and settlements along the Mississippi, the Great Lakes, and Acadia would not be sufficient proof against English encroachments, and with domestic interests directed elsewhere, there was no vigorous government support for colonization, comparatively few colonists, and thus few official records of emigration. In any case, as George Reaman waggishly observes in *The Trail of the Huguenots,* "Frenchmen do not migrate readily."[27]

Such records as we possess, however, deal mainly with the migration and settlement of French Protestants, or Huguenots. During the half-century that preceded the revocation of the Edict of Nantes (1685), the decree which for over eighty years protected French Protestants from persecution, Huguenots had emigrated voluntarily to the French West Indies, or Lesser Antilles, settling principally on the islands of St. Christopher, Guadeloupe, and Martinique. Here they prospered in trade and commerce and practiced their religion in relative peace. With the Revocation, however, the government of Louis XIV instituted a program of compulsory transportation for persons sentenced to penal servitude on account of their religion. During the two years in which this practice appears to have been in force, an indeterminate number of Huguenots were shipped to the French islands, many of whom subsequently removed to Massachusetts, New York, or South Carolina. "Between the month of September, 1686, and the beginning of the year 1688," writes Charles Baird in the *History of the Huguenot Emigration to America,* "as many as ten vessels sailed from Marseilles, most of them bound for Martinique, and carrying over one thousand Huguenots, men and women."[28] Although accounts are incomplete, the total number of involuntary emigrants embarking from French ports during this period must have been considerable.

But besides those who went voluntarily or involuntarily to the West Indies and later removed to the mainland, there were many others who embarked from European and British ports and sailed direct to the American colonies where they were warmly welcomed. In South Carolina Huguenots settled principally on the Santee River, in the Orange Quarter, and in Charleston; in Virginia they congregated in Manakin Town in Henrico County; in New York there were settlements of Huguenots in New Paltz, New Rochelle, Manhattan, Long Island, and Staten Island; and in New England they put down roots in

Boston and Oxford in Massachusetts, and, for a time, in Narragansett in Rhode Island. Few of the existing records, however, other than the transport lists for Manakin Town in 1700 and the lists of members of the Petit-Guérard party bound for South Carolina in 1679 aboard the *Richmond*[29] can be classed as passenger lists; but memorials, petitions, financial accounts, and reports relative to the Huguenots can be found in the Public Record Office, for England had offered a haven to French Protestant refugees as early as 1681 when Charles II was prevailed upon to issue a proclamation promising all distressed Protestants refuge and protection. Four years later, with the revocation of the Edict of Nantes, England reaffirmed its hospitality, even offering to effect the resettlement of selected groups in the colonies. Hence the appearance of Huguenot emigration records—especially the naturalization records in the Patent Rolls—in the Public Record Office. (The majority of the papers relating to the Huguenot emigration to Virginia in 1700, however, are said to be in the Bodleian Library, Oxford.)[30]

Apart from these, and apart from seventeenth-century recruitment lists for settlement in New France (Canada), the most extensive record of French arrivals of the period appears to be the ship lists of passengers sailing from La Rochelle to Louisiana under the auspices of the Company of the Indies, to whom a monopoly of Louisiana had been granted by the King of France in 1717. Included in these remarkable lists, which range in date from 1718 to 1721, are the names of many of those identified with the founding of New Orleans. More significant, perhaps, is the fact that the largest contingent of passengers named in these lists was comprised not of concessionaires, or planters, but of criminals, exiles, and deserters, with data given respecting their ages, places of birth, personal descriptions, and occupations. Banished by order of the King—coincidentally at the very time England had stepped up its own program of enforced transportation—these miscreants must surely have constituted a large proportion of the early settlers of the Mississippi Valley.[31]

Unlike the French and the English, the Dutch of New Netherland had no experience of compulsory transportation, and we look in vain for such records. Nor did their masters in Holland keep embarkation lists or any other records of emigration. In fact, there are few records of any kind relating to New Netherland during the first fifteen years of its existence, though the names of several of the Walloon and Huguenot colonists who first came to the colony aboard the *New Netherland* in 1623 are known.[32] The colony of New Netherland—nominally all the territory lying between the Connecticut River in the north and the Delaware River in the south—was established in 1624 by the Dutch West India Company with the enthusiastic backing of the States-General of the United Netherlands. Even though a Director-General was in place by 1626, assisted by a Council and a Provincial Secretary, the earliest extant records of the colony date only as far back as the year 1638. That any records survive at all is a wonder, for the archives of New Netherland have led a precarious existence. At one time or another they have been under the authority of the Dutch, the English, and the Americans, and those ending up in the possession of the State of New York were rescued only at the eleventh hour from a disastrous fire in the State Library in Albany in 1911—not without serious loss, however. (Many of the Dutch-held records of the West India Company are reported to have been deliberately destroyed in the early part of the nineteenth century.)

Happily, the inhabitants of New Netherland were punctilious to a fault, fond of going to law over the most trifling matter and inclined to an extraordinary degree to protect themselves with all manner of contracts and agreements. And if they were naturally fastidious in their own right, in the face of their suspicions of the New England colonies they were doubly circumspect, so the number of official documents we find after 1638 is quite considerable. To take only one example, prior to 1638 colonists were allowed to choose and take possession only of as much land as they could cultivate, but from 24 June 1638 they were permitted to have land in freehold, with the result that land patents and records of the transfer and ownership of real property begin to show up immediately in the extant records—patents in the land paper books, conveyances in the minutes of the provincial secretary. Until the final takeover of the colony by the English in 1674, the council minutes and registers of the provincial secretary provide a wonderfully detailed record of the executive and judicial decisions affecting the colony as a whole, while court records and notarial registers give us an insight into the workings of local jurisdictions and furnish an extraordinary picture of the colonists themselves. But the fact remains that there are few emigration records, very few records of passenger arrivals, and only two or three authentic passenger lists.

The best known record of the period is, technically, neither a record of emigration nor a passenger list as such, though a number of writers have described it as the only existing record of passengers of the entire Dutch period. It is actually an account book recording the names of persons who owed money to the West India Company for their passage to New Netherland during the period from 1654 to 1664.[33] It lists passengers by ship and by date, giving their occupations and places of origin, and is thought to have been compiled from the West India Company's records on the orders of the English, who had confiscated the Company's property in New Netherland when the Dutch first capitulated in 1664. Whatever its precise origins, the account book does not contain complete lists of passengers but only such as were indebted to the West India Company. Yet it is by far the largest collection of Dutch passenger records known to exist. A similar list concerning passengers on the ship *Rensselaerswyck* in 1636/37 is noted among the Rensselaerswyck manuscripts at the New York State Library. A single list only, it is in fact a memorandum naming persons who were indebted to the owners of the *Rensselaerswyck* for their board, some thirty-three men, women, and children.[34] Three other brief lists, deposited not among the extant papers of the West India Company at the Central Archives in the Hague but in the Amsterdam City Archives, concern passengers bound for New Amstel on the Delaware (known as New Sweden before the Dutch took it over in 1655). Two lists of passengers for separate sailings of the *Purmerlander Kerck* (Purmerland Church) in 1661 and 1662, and one very brief list of persons aboard the *Gulden Arent* (Golden Eagle) in 1662, are apparently all that can be found in the archives of this city, which exercised control of the South River colony from 1661 to 1664.[35] These are at present the only passenger lists of the New Netherland period known to be on file in Dutch archives, though perhaps there are others which are as yet untranslated.

On the subject of New Sweden, we might point out that passenger lists and emigration records in the Royal Archives in Stockholm have been translated by Amandus Johnson in *The Swedish Settlements on the Delaware 1638-1664*, 2 vols. (1911; reprint, Baltimore: Genealogical Publishing Company, 1969), a work so well known as to require little amplification here. It is sufficient to note that in Appendix B —"Lists of Officers, Soldiers, Servants and Settlers in New Sweden, 1638-1656"— there is a list of the male inhabitants of New Sweden,

1643-44, a roll of the people who were alive in New Sweden on 1 March 1648, with details of ships that brought them and dates of their arrival, and a list of settlers in the colony in 1654-55. Passengers in the fourth expedition to New Sweden in the *Kalmar Nyckel* and the *Charitas* (1641), and some in the sixth expedition in the *Fama* (1643-44) and the tenth expedition in the *Örn* (1654), are identified elsewhere in the text.

Partial lists of passengers sailing on the *Kalmar Nyckel* in the second expedition to New Sweden (1640) and on the *Kalmar Nyckel* or the *Charitas* in the third expedition (1641) have been compiled from contemporary sources by Peter S. Craig, an authority on the demography of New Sweden, and published as an appendix in C. A. Weslager's *A Man and His Ship: Peter Minuit and the Kalmar Nyckel* (Wilmington, Del.: Kalmar Nyckel Foundation, 1990). The object of the first expedition of the *Kalmar Nyckel* (1638) was to stake out a Swedish settlement on the Delaware, but the next three expeditions, bringing not only Swedish settlers but Finnish and some Dutch as well, were decisive in stabilizing the colony. Altogether there were twelve expeditions to New Sweden in the seventeen years of its existence, and the four voyages of the *Kalmar Nyckel* stand as milestones in the convulsive history of this long-forgotten colony.

PUBLISHED GUIDES

For all the wealth of data in British archives (and to a lesser extent Continental archives)—in ecclesiastical and state documents, in court records and port books, and in petitions, diaries, and official correspondence—there is nothing remotely resembling a continuous record of emigration, certainly nothing like the continuous record of immigration known to exist for the bulk of the nineteenth century in American archives. Nevertheless, owing to the comparatively limited immigration that took place during the colonial and early federal periods, it is generally accepted that we have evidence of the departure or arrival of a significant proportion of these early immigrants, although no precise figure can ever be established. So much attention has centered on the immigrants of this period, in fact, that practically every known record of migration, every passenger list—original or synthetic—has appeared in print. Whether they may be considered the most important record source in immigration research is perhaps debatable, but ships' passenger lists and related records usually provide the first, often the only, evidence of an immigrant on American soil, and provide the only conclusive proof of his passage. Where other records founder on insights, ships' passenger lists suggest flesh and personality, and summon to mind a catalogue of the political, economic, and religious forces that inspired European emigration. They cannot generally be said to convey any sense of what a passenger was like in feature or in habits, since at best they are mere inventories of human cargo, but they are manna to the researcher who strains after any remote link to the old world. Typically, they consist of an itemization of names, ages, sex, occupations, and places of origin and destination, and they sometimes contain references to financial circumstances and reasons for emigrating, but little else. Yet there is so much that is momentous and epochal in these lists that the researcher can almost divine in them an echo of history.

Since the middle of the nineteenth century ships' passenger lists have appeared in print with increasing frequency. They have been so painstakingly reconstructed from original sources, copied, re-copied, and finally published in a profusion of books, monographs, and articles, that a very considerable literature has developed on the subject. So formidable had this literature become that as long ago as 1937 Harold Lancour of the New York Public Library concluded that it required some form of bibliographical organization. His *Passenger Lists of Ships Coming to North America, 1607-1825: A Bibliography* united hundreds of disparate threads and gave permanent definition to this difficult and unwieldy body of material. While there was no official register of immigrants of the seventeenth and eighteenth centuries, no master list, there was now at least a book that delineated every known published list of immigrants.

In view of the rapid growth in passenger list publications, however, the last edition of this pioneering work, the third, revised and enlarged by Richard J. Wolfe in 1963 under the title *A Bibliography of Ship Passenger Lists 1538-1825,* soon became obsolete, and by the late 1970s it was apparent that the recent proliferation of books, papers, and articles had made a nonsense of the established canon. Recognizing the heightened activity in the field and the need to bring the Lancour work up to date by providing a bibliographical record of all passenger lists and immigration records, especially those published since 1963, P. William Filby produced his *Passenger and Immigration Lists Bibliography 1538-1900* in 1981, a *Supplement* in 1984, and a second, cumulative edition in 1988.[36] A far more ambitious work than Lancour, containing a total of 2,600 entries against Lancour's 262, and extending the period of coverage well beyond Lancour's 1825 cut-off date, this new bibliography not only brings the Lancour work current but corrects some of the inaccuracies of that earlier work and supplies some of its surprising omissions. Its numerous citations to out-of-the-way publications such as foreign-language journals make it an even more useful work. It reaches across the entire spectrum of known publications, from society yearbooks and annuals to learned journals and reviews, from books and newspapers to pamphlets and newsletters, and provides, as near as possible, an exhaustive list of published ships' passenger lists and immigration records from the seventeenth century to the beginning of the twentieth century.

Anyone pursuing a line of enquiry in this area would be well advised to acquaint himself with the Filby work before proceeding on to the original records. Certainly anyone wishing to know what already exists or, by elimination, what does not exist, must know his Filby. Its greatest strength is in its coverage of pre-nineteenth-century immigration records, since records of this earlier period, as far as we know, have nearly all been published. Naturally, with scholars beginning to chip away at the mountainous records of the nineteenth century, their publications, to date, are also cited in the bibliography. The literature grows by the day, and before long Filby itself will need augmenting or replacing, but in the meantime it is the only reliable guide to this indispensable resource.

Just as the Filby bibliography is a guide to published ships' passenger lists and immigration records, a companion work, also compiled by Filby but with the assistance of Mary K. Meyer, stands as an index, and it is recommended as a useful place in which to begin research on immigration records for the period prior to the nineteenth century. *Passenger and Immigration Lists Index* (3 vols., 1981), with its annual and cumulated *Supplements,* is an attempt to merge into one alphabet the names of all immigrants mentioned in the various works cited in the bibliography.[37] Except that it falls short of its goal to index all published arrival records, which is inevitable considering the voluminous data presented in certain works treating nineteenth-century immigrants, it is the most convenient tool available to help determine the identities of immigrants of the period from 1607 to 1800. It is not absolutely comprehensive even for this period, but the enormous opportunities presented by the two million names that have been indexed to date can't be overlooked.

NOTES

1. The order was enacted into law at a session of the General Assembly in March 1632 and re-enacted at a session of the Grand Assembly the following September. See William W. Hening, *The Statutes at Large; Being a Collection of all the Laws of Virginia, from the First Session of the Legislature, in the Year 1619* (Richmond, 1809), 1: 166, 191-92. It's entirely possible that these records of arrival—if they ever existed—were destroyed in the burning of the State court building in Richmond in 1865, as the majority of General Court minutes after 1632 were lost in this conflagration.

2. The original records are located in the Historical Society of Pennsylvania in Philadelphia, and a contemporary copy of the Bucks County register is said to be in the Bucks County Historical Society at Doylestown. The registers in the possession of the Historical Society of Pennsylvania have been transcribed and published by Hannah Benner Roach in "The Philadelphia and Bucks County Registers of Arrivals, Compared, Corrected and Re-transcribed," in *Passengers and Ships Prior to 1684,* edited by Walter Lee Sheppard, Jr., Publications of the Welcome Society of Pennsylvania, vol. 1 (Baltimore: Genealogical Publishing Company, 1970), 159-75. For a full discussion and exploitation of the registers see George E. McCracken, *The Welcome Claimants, Proved, Disproved and Doubtful,* Publications of the Welcome Society of Pennsylvania, vol. 2 (Baltimore: Genealogical Publishing Company, 1970).

3. The lists of passengers on the *Ann* and the *Bonny Bess,* recorded in the minutes of the General Court for 1622 to 1629, are located in the Thomas Jefferson Papers in the Library of Congress. They have been printed in H. R. McIlwaine, ed., *Minutes of the Council and General Court of Colonial Virginia,* 2nd ed. (Richmond: Virginia State Library, 1979), 6. Another version of the lists, transcribed by Lothrop Withington and annotated by William G. Stanard, appears in "Minutes of the Council and General Court, 1622-1624," *Virginia Magazine of History and Biography* 19 (1911): 131-34.

4. The two "Divisions" are printed in *Records of the Colony of New Plymouth in New England,* ed. Nathaniel B. Shurtleff and David Pulsifer, 12 vols. (Boston, 1861), 12: 4-6, 9-13. They are also printed,

with additional background material, in Eugene A. Stratton, *Plymouth Colony: Its History & People 1620-1691* (Salt Lake City: Ancestry Publishing, 1986). In addition, they provide the basis for some of the conclusions reached by Charles Edward Banks concerning the identities and relationships of the Pilgrims in *The English Ancestry and Homes of the Pilgrim Fathers* (1929; reprint, Baltimore: Genealogical Publishing Company, 1962).

5. The impost records for 1715-16 and 1762-69 are thought to be in the Boston City Archives, but as the collection is uncalendared and the archives itself presently in disarray, this has not been possible to verify. The records are published in *A Volume of Records Relating to the Early History of Boston Containing Miscellaneous Papers*, Registry Department of the City of Boston (29th in the series formerly called *Record Commissioners' Reports*), Doc. 100 (Boston, 1900), 229-317. This was later excerpted and reprinted as *Port Arrivals and Immigrants to the City of Boston 1715-1716 and 1762-1769* (Baltimore: Genealogical Publishing Company, 1973). Impost records for 1712 have been published in "Passengers to America," *New England Historical and Genealogical Register* 30-33 (1876-79). According to this article the originals are in the collection of the New England Historic Genealogical Society in Boston, but a recent search at the Society has failed to locate them.

6. Ralph B. Strassburger, *Pennsylvania German Pioneers: A Publication of the Original Lists of Arrivals in the Port of Philadelphia from 1727 to 1808,* ed. William J. Hinke, 3 vols. (Norristown, Pa.: Pennsylvania German Society, 1934; reprint (in 2 vols.), Baltimore: Genealogical Publishing Company, 1966). Vol. 2, containing facsimiles of all the signatures to the oaths of allegiance and abjuration, was not included in GPC's 1966 reprint but has since been published by Picton Press of Camden, Maine and by Genealogical Books in Print of Springfield, Virginia. See also Friedrich Krebs, "Annotations to Strassburger and Hinke's Pennsylvania German Pioneers," *Pennsylvania Genealogical Magazine* 21 (1960): 235-48.

7. *Cavaliers and Pioneers: Abstracts of Virginia Land Patents and Grants 1623-1666,* comp. Nell M. Nugent (1934; reprint, Baltimore: Genealogical Publishing Company, 1963), 1:xxv.

8. The earlier records are published in George W. Neible, "Servants and Apprentices Bound and Assigned Before James Hamilton, Mayor

of Philadelphia, 1745 [-1746]," *Pennsylvania Magazine of History and Biography* 30-32 (1906-08). The records for 1771-73, in the possession of the American Philosophical Society in Philadelphia, appear in *Record of Indentures of Individuals Bound Out as Apprentices, Servants, Etc. and of German and Other Redemptioners in the Office of the Mayor of the City of Philadelphia, October 3, 1771 to October 5, 1773* (1907; reprint, Baltimore: Genealogical Publishing Company, 1973). Records for December 5, 1772 to May 21, 1773, located in the manuscript department of the Historical Society of Pennsylvania (considerably less complete than the records in the American Philosophical Society), have been published in "Record of Servants and Apprentices Bound and Assigned Before Hon. John Gibson, Mayor of Philadelphia," *Pennsylvania Magazine of History and Biography* 33-34 (1909-10).

9.   There are several published collections of Quaker certificates of removal, two of the best known compiled by Albert Cook Myers: "List of Certificates of Removal from Ireland Received at the Monthly Meetings of Friends in Pennsylvania, 1682-1750," in *Immigration of the Irish Quakers into Pennsylvania 1682-1750* (1902; reprint, Baltimore: Genealogical Publishing Company, 1969), 277-390; and *Quaker Arrivals at Philadelphia 1682-1750; Being a List of Certificates of Removal Received at Philadelphia Monthly Meeting of Friends* (1902; reprint, Baltimore: Genealogical Publishing Company, 1957).

10.   Letters of denization and naturalization were granted by royal prerogative and by special acts of Parliament and colonial legislatures. Those granted in pursuance of an act of Parliament in 1740 and recorded in register books kept by the Commissioners for Trade and Plantations in London have been published in M. S. Giuseppi, *Naturalizations of Foreign Protestants in the American and West Indian Colonies (Pursuant to Statute 13 George II, c. 7)* (1921; reprint, Baltimore: Genealogical Publishing Company, 1964). Supplementing the information in the Giuseppi book (for New York) is Richard J. Wolfe, "The Colonial Naturalization Act of 1740; With a List of Persons Naturalized in New York Colony, 1740-1769," *New York Genealogical and Biographical Record* 94 (1963): 132-47. See also Kenneth Scott and Kenn Stryker-Rodda, *Denizations, Naturalizations, and Oaths of Allegiance in Colonial New York* (Baltimore: Genealogical Publishing Company, 1975).

Of the extant size rolls, those in the George Washington Papers in the Library of Congress are perhaps the best known. They have been transcribed and printed most recently in Murtie J. Clark, *Colonial Soldiers of the South, 1732-1774* (Baltimore: Genealogical Publishing Company, 1983) and Lloyd D. Bockstruck, *Virginia's Colonial Soldiers* (Baltimore: Genealogical Publishing Company, 1988). For translations of the New Netherland records see the series *New York Historical Manuscripts. Dutch,* ed. Peter R. Christoph, Charles T. Gehring et al., published under the direction of the Holland Society of New York (1974–). See also *Documents Relative to the Colonial History of the State of New York,* ed. E. B. O'Callaghan (vols. 1-11) and Berthold Fernow (vols. 12-15), Albany, 1857-83.

11. For testimonials printed in the *Pennsylvania Packet and Daily Advertiser* in 1789—paid for and signed by the passengers—see Hannah Benner Roach, "Post-Revolutionary Arrivals in the Delaware River," *Pennsylvania Genealogical Magazine* 28 (1973): 81-85. Testimonials carried in the *Packet* from 1785 to 1788 are published in "Post-Revolutionary Arrivals at the Port of Philadelphia," *Pennsylvania Genealogical Magazine* 26 (1970): 179-82, 263-66. Two other newspaper lists, originally printed in the *Delaware Gazette* in 1789 and 1790, are published in articles contributed by P. William Filby in the *Maryland and Delaware Genealogist* 20 (1979): 13-14. See also letters of thanks printed in the *Belfast* [Ireland] *News Letter,* published in Jean Stephenson, *Scotch-Irish Migration to South Carolina, 1772* (Strasburg, Va.: Shenandoah Publishing House, 1971), 29-35. For announcements of new arrivals and ads placed by recent arrivals trying to locate friends and relatives, see, in particular, Edward W. Hocker, *Genealogical Data Relating to the German Settlers of Pennsylvania and Adjacent Territory From Advertisements in German Newspapers Published in Philadelphia and Germantown, 1743-1800* (Baltimore: Genealogical Publishing Company, 1980).

12. 3 vols. (Richmond, 1934, 1977, 1979). Vol. 1, originally published by the Dietz Printing Company in 1934, covers the years 1623 to 1666. Vol. 2 (1977) and vol. 3 (1979), published by the Virginia State Library, cover 1666-1695 and 1695-1732 respectively.

13. Jean Stephenson's *Scotch-Irish Migration to South Carolina, 1772* (see note 11) is a rather more detailed compilation of materials relating to the emigration of one specific group—the Rev. William Martin and his five shiploads of settlers from Ballymoney, Co. Antrim.

14. A list of about fifty men and women sent for plantation in

Virginia, found among the Smyth of Nibley papers in the New York Public Library, is printed in Susan M. Kingsbury, *The Records of the Virginia Company of London,* 4 vols. (Washington, D.C.: Government Printing Office, 1906-35), 3:396-97.

15. *Kingsbury* 1 (1906): 77.

16. *Kingsbury* 4 (1935): 551-59 (from records of the Virginia Company in the Library of Congress). Another version is printed in John Camden Hotten, *The Original Lists of Persons of Quality* (1874; reprint, Baltimore: Genealogical Publishing Company, 1974), 266-74.

17. For a list of prisoners taken at the Battle of Dunbar and subsequently deported to the colonies, see Charles Edward Banks, "Scotch Prisoners Deported to New England by Cromwell, 1651-52," *Massachusetts Historical Society Proceedings* 61 (1928): 4-29. Lists of rebels deported in the aftermath of the abortive 1685 rebellion can be found in Hotten (see above), 315-44. See also Colin Campbell, "Deportations from Scotland, 1685," *New England Historical and Genealogical Register* 114 (1960): 150-51. Covenanters transported on the *Henry and Francis* to Perth Amboy, New Jersey in 1685 are listed—among other places—in S. Helen Fields, "Covenanters and the Work of Rev. John Cuthbertson," *National Genealogical Society Quarterly* 21 (1933): 16-18. Scottish prisoners transported after the siege of Preston in 1715 are listed in Cecil Headlam, *Calendar of State Papers, Colonial Series, America and West Indies, January 1716-July 1717* (London: His Majesty's Stationery Office, 1930), 29: 166-71. Publications concerning the deportation of Scottish prisoners in the wake of the 1745 uprising are so numerous that it is suggested only that a start be made with David Dobson, *Directory of Scots Banished to the American Plantations, 1650-1775* (Baltimore: Genealogical Publishing Company, 1983).

18. Quoted from *Calendar of State Papers, Colonial Series, 1611,* in Peter W. Coldham, *The Complete Book of Emigrants in Bondage, 1614-1775* (Baltimore: Genealogical Publishing Company, 1988), p. x.

19. Baltimore: Genealogical Publishing Company, 1988 (as above). The two previous editions of this work were published under different titles, first, *English Convicts in Colonial America,* 2 vols. [vol. 1,

Middlesex; vol. 2, London] (New Orleans: Polyanthos, Inc., 1974-76); second, *Bonded Passengers to America*, 9 vols. in 3 (Baltimore: Genealogical Publishing Company, 1983). This edition incorporated the two volumes of 1974 and 1976 for Middlesex and London, added records from the Assize and Palatinate courts for the rest of the counties of England, and was introduced by a history of transportation (since revised and published separately as *Emigrants in Chains, 1607-1776* [Baltimore: Genealogical Publishing Company, 1992]). Omitting the history, the 1988 edition (in one volume) incorporates the previous records, adds records of the Courts of Quarter Session, and integrates all the records into a single alphabetical sequence. Recently opened records in the Bristol Record Office, revealing previously unknown (but long suspected) criminal transportation records, along with certain records which escaped detection during Mr. Coldham's first round of researches, are published in *Supplement to The Complete Book of Emigrants in Bondage, 1614-1775* (Baltimore: Genealogical Publishing Company, 1992).

20. For transcriptions of these records see, respectively, Walter A. Knittle, *Early Eighteenth Century Palatine Emigration* (1937; reprint, Baltimore: Genealogical Publishing Company, 1965) and John Tribbeko and George Ruperti, "Lists of Germans from the Palatinate Who Came to England in 1709," *New York Genealogical and Biographical Record* 40-41 (1909-10); E. Merton Coulter and Albert B. Saye, *A List of the Early Settlers of Georgia* [from the Egmont manuscripts at the University of Georgia] (1949, 1967; reprint, Baltimore: Genealogical Publishing Company, 1983) and George F. Jones, *The Germans of Colonial Georgia, 1733-1783* (Baltimore: Genealogical Publishing Company, 1986); and St. Julien R. Childs, "The Petit-Guérard Colony," *South Carolina Historical and Genealogical Magazine* 43 (1942): 1-17, 88-97. For publications pertaining to the naturalization of foreign-born Protestants, see note 10.

21. Abstracts of the records of the Prerogative Court of Canterbury and the High Court of Admiralty with reference to colonial America have been published by Peter W. Coldham in *English Estates of American Colonists: American Wills and Administrations in the Prerogative Court of Canterbury*, 3 vols. [i.e. 1610-1699, 1700-1799, 1800-1858] (Baltimore: Genealogical Publishing Company, 1980-81); and *English Adventurers and Emigrants: Abstracts of Examinations in the High Court of Admiralty with Reference to Colonial America*, 2 vols. [i.e. 1609-1660, 1661-1733] (Baltimore: Genea-

logical Publishing Company, 1984-85). The first named work has since been superseded by Coldham's own *American Wills & Administrations in the Prerogative Court of Canterbury, 1610-1857* (Baltimore: Genealogical Publishing Company, 1989), which has been augmented by yet another Coldham work, *American Wills Proved in London, 1611-1775* (Baltimore: Genealogical Publishing Company, 1992).

22. Best known in this area is the work of Marion R. Balderston whose reconstruction of passenger lists from the 1681-83 port records of London, Bristol, and Liverpool should be required reading for students of colonial emigration. See, in particular, "William Penn's Twenty-Three Ships, With Notes on Some of Their Passengers" and "Pennsylvania's 1683 Ships and Some of Their Passengers," in *Passengers and Ships Prior to 1684,* edited by Walter Lee Sheppard, Jr., Publications of the Welcome Society of Pennsylvania, vol. 1 (Baltimore: Genealogical Publishing Company, 1970), 27-69, 75-120. See also Peter W. Coldham, "Passengers and Ships to America, 1618-1668" (Genealogical Gleanings in England), *National Genealogical Society Quarterly* 71 (1983): 163-92, 284-96; 72 (1984): 132-45.

23. The English records have been transcribed in Gerald Fothergill, *Emigrants from England 1773-1776* (1913; reprint, Baltimore: Genealogical Publishing Company, 1964), and the Scottish records in Viola R. Cameron, *Emigrants from Scotland to America, 1774-1775* (1930; reprint, Baltimore: Genealogical Publishing Company, 1959). According to Prof. Bernard Bailyn, both transcriptions are seriously flawed by errors of commission and omission. See Bailyn's brilliant, multi-dimensional study of the original records in *Voyagers to the West: A Passage in the Peopling of America on the Eve of the Revolution* (New York: Alfred A. Knopf, 1986). Not itself a transcription of the records, the Bailyn work is nevertheless the most detailed and comprehensive analysis of a single group of emigration records ever published. After the publication of the Bailyn work, the indefatigable Peter Coldham re-transcribed the English records, now published as *Emigrants from England to the American Colonies, 1773-1776* (Baltimore: Genealogical Publishing Company, 1988), showing port by port, in order of departure, the names of ships and the name of each emigrant, including his town or county of residence in England, his occupation, his age, and his destination in the colonies. (A card index to the English records is located in the Public Record Office at Kew.)

24. These have been published elsewhere, however. See James R. Brandow, *Omitted Chapters from Hotten's Original Lists of Persons of Quality* (Baltimore: Genealogical Publishing Company, 1982).

25. Most recently transcribed and published in Peter W. Coldham, *The Bristol Registers of Servants Sent to Foreign Plantations, 1654-1686* (Baltimore: Genealogical Publishing Company, 1988), which substantially improves on R. Hargreaves-Mawdsley's faulty *Bristol and America: A Record of the First Settlers in the Colonies of North America 1654-1685* (London, 1929). Other publications listing indentured servants bound from England include: Michael Ghirelli, *A List of Emigrants from England to America 1682-1692* [from the Lord Mayor's Waiting Books in the Records Office of the Corporation of London] (Baltimore: Magna Carta Book Company, 1968); Cregoe D. P. Nicholson, *Some Early Emigrants to America* [from records dated 1683-84 in the Middlesex Guildhall, London] (1955-60; reprint, Baltimore: Genealogical Publishing Company, 1965); Elizabeth French, *List of Emigrants to America from Liverpool 1697-1707* (1913; reprint, Baltimore: Genealogical Publishing Company, 1962); Jack Kaminkow and Marion Kaminkow, *A List of Emigrants from England to America 1718-1759* [from records in the Guildhall, London] (Baltimore: Magna Carta Book Company, 1981); John Wareing, *Emigrants to America: Indentured Servants Recruited in London 1718-1733* [from a register kept in the Records Office of the Corporation of London] (Baltimore: Genealogical Publishing Company, 1985); and Peter W. Coldham, *Child Apprentices in America from Christ's Hospital, London, 1617-1778* [from the "Children's Registers" in the manuscript department of the Guildhall, London] (Baltimore: Genealogical Publishing Company, 1990).

26. Records of Emigrants from Zurich, Bern, and Basel—from church, state, and private archives—have been collected and published in *Lists of Swiss Emigrants in the Eighteenth Century to the American Colonies,* ed. Gaius M. Brumbaugh and Albert B. Faust, 2 vols. [vol. 1, Zurich, 1734-44; vol. 2, Bern, 1706-95, Basel, 1734-94] (Washington, D.C.: National Genealogical Society, 1920-25). Additions and corrections appear in a review essay by Leo Schelbert, "Notes on Lists of Swiss Emigrants," *National Genealogical Society Quarterly* 60 (1972): 36-46. The two volumes and the Schelbert article were combined and reprinted in a single volume by the Genealogical Publishing Company in 1976.

27.   *The Trail of the Huguenots in Europe, the United States, South Africa and Canada* (1963; reprint (with additions and corrections), Baltimore: Genealogical Publishing Company, 1966), 155.

28.   2 vols. (1885; reprint (2 vols. in 1), Baltimore: Genealogical Publishing Company, 1973), 1: 221.

29.   Records of the Manakin Town transports are published in Robert A. Brock, *Documents, Chiefly Unpublished, Relating to the Huguenot Emigration to Virginia and to the Settlement at Manakin-Town* (1886; reprint, Baltimore: Genealogical Publishing Company, 1962); for lists of passengers on the *Richmond* see the article by St. Julien R. Childs cited in note 20 above.

30.   Brock, *Huguenot Emigration to Virginia,* 9.

31.   Located in the Paris Archives, the La Rochelle embarkation lists have been transcribed and published in Neil J. Toups, *Mississippi Valley Pioneers* (Lafayette, La.: Neilson Publishing Company [1970]). Another version, less complete than Toups, is published in Albert Laplace Dart, trans., "Ship Lists of Passengers Leaving France for Louisiana, 1718-1724," *Louisiana Historical Quarterly* 14 (1931), 15 (1932), 21 (1938). A recently discovered list of prospective brides (or deportees) sent over on the ship *Baleine* in 1721 from the infamous Hôpital-Général de la Salpêtrière of Paris has been published in the *National Genealogical Society Quarterly* 75 (1987): 303-05.

32.   For a conjectural list of the first settlers of New Netherland, see Baird, *Huguenot Emigration to America* 1: 172-75.

33.   Several translations of those portions of the account book comprising lists of indebted passengers have been published, the most accurate translation believed to be Arnold J. F. van Laer, "List of Passengers, 1654 to 1664" (Passengers to New Netherland), in *Year Book of the Holland Society of New York* (1902), 1-28. Additional material, from the notes of historian James Riker, appears in Rosalie Fellows Bailey, "Emigrants to New Netherland: Account Book 1654 to 1664," *New York Genealogical and Biographical Record* 94 (1963): 193-200. The original account book is in the New York State Library in Albany.

34.   Translated and published in Arnold J. F. van Laer, "Settlers of

the Colony of Rensselaerswyck, 1637," *New York Genealogical and Biographical Record* 49 (1918): 365-67. This supplements the passenger list of the *Rensselaerswyck* printed in "Settlers of Rensselaerswyck 1630-1658" [pp. 805-46 of van Laer's *Van Rensselaer Bowier Manuscripts*] (1908; reprint, Baltimore: Genealogical Publishing Company, 1965).

35. Translated and published in A. R. Dunlap, "Three Lists of Passengers to New Amstel," *Delaware History* 8 (1959): 310-11.

36. Published by Gale Research Company of Detroit. The subtitle reads: *Being a Guide to Published Lists of Arrivals in the United States and Canada.*

37. *Passenger and Immigration Lists Index: A Guide to Published Arrival Records of about 500,000 Passengers Who Came to the United States and Canada in the Seventeenth, Eighteenth, and Nineteenth Centuries,* 3 vols. (Detroit: Gale Research Company, 1981). Annual *Supplements* have been published since 1982, and *Cumulated Supplements* for 1982-85 (4 vols.) and 1986-90 (3 vols.) have also been published.

THE BEGINNING OF FEDERAL
PASSENGER ARRIVAL RECORDS

With minor exceptions, federal passenger arrival records can be said to begin in January 1800—not the great corpus of records we shall come to know as Customs Passenger Lists, but an obscure collection of records known as "baggage lists." Kept primarily by officials at the port of Philadelphia, these improbable records exist in virtual isolation, for no other federal passenger arrival records were maintained at U.S. ports of entry until the year 1820. Admittedly, a small number of records developed at other levels of government or outside of public authority are known to exist for portions of the 1800-1820 period, notably records of "foreign" arrivals at the port of Philadelphia, which extend to the beginning of 1808, and lists of Irish passenger arrivals from 1811 to 1817, published intermittently in the New York weekly *The Shamrock or Hibernian Chronicle,*[1] but of all the known records of immigration for this period, only the Philadelphia baggage lists make any claim to continuity or measure up to our expectations of a first-class body of records. Since they stand at the very head of nineteenth-century immigration records, they make a special claim on our attention and raise a few questions that are worth looking into.

Unlike Customs Passenger Lists, which were an outgrowth of legislation framed for the purpose of placing controls on immigration, baggage lists originated from an act of Congress that had no bearing on immigration other than the benign intention to exempt incoming passengers from paying duty on their personal belongings. A minor provision of this act—*An Act to Regulate the Collection of Duties on Imports and Tonnage* (2 March 1799)—instructed ships' captains to draw up manifests with the names of passengers carrying baggage, instructing them to

> have on board a manifest, or manifests, in writing, signed by such master or other person . . . together with the name or names of the several passengers on board the said ship or vessel, distinguishing whether cabin or steerage passengers, or both, with their baggage, specifying the number and description of packages belonging to each respectively. (*section 23*)

While a later section of the act explained:

> That . . . the wearing apparel, and other personal baggage, and the tools or implements of a mechanical trade only, of persons who arrive in the United States, shall be free and exempted from duty. (*section 46*)

Here, in the middle of a tariff act designed to consolidate the various laws which had been enacted since 1790 for laying and collecting duties on imports and tonnage—an act creating customs districts, ports of entry, and ports of delivery, showing the jurisdiction of each, calling for the appointment of customs collectors, naval officers, and surveyors, prescribing the exact form of cargo manifests and other documents to be deposited with customs officers by ships' masters, and apportioning a great multitude of exacting and overlapping tasks—here did the mandate for keeping lists of passengers first emerge. With the exception of the short-lived Alien Act of 25 June 1798, this was the first official measure to call for a listing or a report of incoming passengers. This being said, it must be admitted straightaway that Philadelphia was virtually alone in complying with the law, for with the exception of a small number of baggage lists found among the records of the New Orleans customs district—spotty lists for 1813 and 1815—and the district of Alexandria, Virginia (more haphazard even than New Orleans), no other port of entry on the Atlantic or the Gulf appears to have maintained the specific type of records called for in the 1799 act.

It's possible of course that baggage lists were deposited at other ports of entry and subsequently lost or destroyed, but circumstantial evidence suggests otherwise. One has to wonder, for example, at the promulgation of new laws and the welter of federal regulations that had to be complied with by the several states, each of them wary and jealous of federal authority, and whether such laws could be observed in all their particulars; whether in fact there was a disposition to comply with every iota of such a law as that of 2 March 1799 or, in the interest of expedience, to ignore those provisions which seemed at best incidental to the purpose of the act. And it is arguable whether the *Act to Regulate the Collection of Duties on Imports and Tonnage* wasn't excessive in its requirements, saddling customs officials with responsibility for keeping a multitude of records such as manifests, certificates of tonnage and freight, itemizations of cargo, estimates and appraisals, consignment documents, landing permits, and a host of related items— all requiring scrupulous attention to detail. In view of these burdens even Philadelphia officials must have been tempted to deviate from a strict interpretation of the law. Section 46, for example, contained a provision stipulating that a separate declarations form be completed by passengers with non-dutiable goods and filed at the port of entry with the customs collector. But evidence suggests that Philadelphia customs officials accepted the signed cargo manifests (per section 23) and winked at the tiresome details of section 46, for only a small number of these declarations forms exist. Why, we might ask, would customs officials at other ports of entry not adopt similar expedients and even disregard certain provisions of the act wholesale? The enumeration of passengers and baggage was certainly not the object of the act, so why not ignore those provisions altogether?

There may even have been a precedent for it. Less than a year earlier Congress had adopted the controversial Alien Act, the second of the Alien and Sedition laws, an act so partisan and so bitterly contested that written into it was the date of its own expiration—two years from its adoption on June 25, 1798. The third section of this act ordered:

> That every master or commander of any ship or vessel, which shall come into port . . . shall, immediately on his arrival, make report in writing to the collector or other chief officer of the customs of such port, of all aliens, if any, on board his vessel, specifying their names, age, the place of nativity, the country from which they shall have come, the nation to which they belong and owe allegiance, their

occupation, and a description of their persons. . . . And it
shall be the duty of such collector, or other officer of the
customs, forthwith to transmit to the office of the Department of State true copies of all such returns.

Using language that was to become a model for later enactments, this
was the first federal law to call for the keeping of passenger arrival
records—lists of aliens, at any rate—along with the requirement that
copies of such lists be forwarded to the State Department, this latter,
incidentally, a procedure followed in one form or another until 1874
when the Bureau of Customs was organized as a division of the
Treasury Department. There could be no misunderstanding this provision of the act nor any confusion regarding the penalties for failure
to comply. Yet non-compliance may have been universal, because no
trace of these lists can be found today apart from nine fragmentary lists
of aliens disembarking at Salem and Beverly in Massachusetts (now
located among the records of the U.S. Customs Service in the National
Archives). Commenting on this act, and directing attention in particular to the Salem and Beverly lists, Meredith Colket, formerly on
the staff of the National Archives, speculates that most of the alien lists
required by law have been lost or destroyed, and as to baggage lists,
"past generations often did not regard such records as of sufficient
value to be preserved, and it is believed that the records were destroyed
for most ports." [2]

This argument has a suspiciously familiar ring to it, however. It is
often urged with regard to missing records—sometimes quite accu-
rately, as is the case, for example, with the loss and despoliation that
occurred when the British burnt the Capitol and government department buildings in 1814—and it is frequently offered as an explanation
for the missing baggage lists. It is in fact so commonly used to explain
gaps and deficiencies in the public records that it has become an article
of faith. But it's a rather convenient argument and we are perhaps a bit
too inclined to accept it at face value. Certainly some degree of loss
and destruction is inevitable—a dead certainty in the case of the evolv-
ing bureaucracies of the new federal government—but it strains
credulity to think that the lists of aliens, almost without exception, were
lost or destroyed at each of the nearly 100 official ports of entry and
that the copies sent to the State Department met a similar fate. It's at
least equally plausible that these records never existed at all, that they

were kept neither at the ports of entry nor at the State Department. Given the controversial nature of the Alien Act and the fact that it was to remain in force for only two years when it would certainly take months to bring it into operation, it is unlikely that the section of the act requiring a report of alien passengers would be pursued with any vigor. Extending this line of argument just a bit further, seeing that penalties for non-compliance would have been difficult to enforce, it might be supposed that section 23 of the act of 1799 could also be ignored with impunity. Of the great multitude of requirements, surely this was one that could be sacrificed to expedience.

This thesis is admittedly speculative, and in the light of later research it may prove erroneous, but in the meantime, in the absence of evidence to the contrary, it is proposed as an explanation for the "loss" both of the lists of aliens and the baggage lists. It does not, however, explain the existence of the Philadelphia baggage lists. For these lists alone, except for the fragmentary New Orleans and Alexandria lists, demonstrate that the requirements of section 23 of the act of 1799 were not meant to be left to the discretion of the customs collectors. Why, then, these Philadelphia lists? Why not New York or Boston or any of a dozen or more ports up and down the coast? Why any lists at all? And if any, why Philadelphia? A definitive answer will probably elude us, but it is reasonable to suppose that since Philadelphia officials were familiar with the practice of collecting passenger lists—had in fact been collecting passenger lists for the better part of a century (see chapter 1)—they above all others would have been prepared to discharge the duties required of them by the new law. It may be as simple as that. Where officials at other major ports of entry might have been daunted or even discomfited by the new law, the authorities in Philadelphia, with their long experience of collecting lists of "foreign" passenger arrivals, merely had to make some adjustments to accommodate and to see to it that customs officers adapted to the new regimen.

Whatever may ultimately prove to be the correct answer, the Philadelphia baggage lists remain something of an oddity. To begin with they appear to have been collected from cargo vessels as distinct from passenger vessels or the less common packet ships, though it is by no means always clear where the distinction lay, since the majority of vessels transporting passengers at this time were converted merchantmen or ordinary cargo vessels which engaged in the carriage of passengers to avoid returning from abroad in ballast. In the vast majority of cases the lists of passengers with baggage were written at the bottom of the cargo manifest, beneath the bill of lading and consignment and usually just above the printed (sometimes handwritten) statement calling for "the names of all passengers, distinguishing whether cabin or steerage passengers, with the description and number of packages containing their baggage, or the tools, or implements of a mechanical trade." Passengers' names were taken down without regard to system, alternately grouped under heads of families and bracketed by "cabin" or "steerage" designations, or recorded randomly without classification of any kind. Less frequently the lists are found on a separate declarations form or on the outside of the folded manifest. Typically, no more than a handful of passengers are named in each list, although longer lists of fifteen or twenty passengers are found, and there are even a few manifests containing as many as two hundred names. Nevertheless, with approximately 40,000 passengers recorded in the 4,767 ship lists for the twenty years from 1800 through 1819, an average of between eight and nine passengers per list gives perhaps a better idea of their range.[3] In general, the lists give every appearance of being hastily written, and they are virtually all couched in the language of an inventory—"John Doe and family, 2 trunks wearing apparel, 2 beds and bedding, 1 writing desk," for example. But a good few are more expansive, dwelling on such items as passengers' ages, nationalities, former places of residence, occupations, destinations, and the names and relationships of accompanying family members—all adventitious, of course, and a further indication that no fixed plan or system was followed.

Since the baggage lists cannot be accepted as representative of the general flow of immigration into the United States during the 1800-1820 period, any patterns that can be extrapolated from them must ultimately be inconclusive. It would appear, though, that some earlier trends in immigration were carried over, for passengers from Germany and Great Britain (the north of Ireland, in particular) continue to predominate. The preference for Pennsylvania shown by both the Ulster Scots and the Rhineland Germans in the eighteenth century is to some extent evident here in the early nineteenth century, perhaps from these groups being long habituated to the idea of Philadelphia as the gateway to America. In Ireland, previously, repressive trade laws, rackrenting, discrimination against Presbyterians by the Test Act, periodic famines and droughts, the consolidation of small holdings for tillage into larger farms for pasturage, high taxes, increasing rents, depressed crop prices, and the general decline in linen manufacturing, the North's main industry, were the principal causes of emigration. In Germany, and to a lesser extent Switzerland, similar conditions obtained, though perhaps in reverse. There, religious and political repression were at first the chief causes for quitting the fatherland, but deteriorating economic conditions came a close second. And to the hard-pressed Ulsterman and the sectarian German there were practical considerations favoring emigration to Pennsylvania. William Penn and his agents had been at work in Ireland and Germany since the late seventeenth century, in the former attracting a number of Quakers into the province with the promise of religious freedom and cheap land; in the latter, as early as 1682, enticing members of various dissenting sects with almost the identical arguments At the same time, Pennsylvania's system of indentured servitude must have been an equally powerful attraction. Judging only from the extant records of servants bound and assigned before the mayors of Philadelphia, thousands of German and Irish immigrants met the cost of their passage by means of contract servitude.

But exactly to what extent the 1800-1820 immigration to Philadelphia mirrored the trends of the eighteenth century, and to what extent the baggage lists are a microcosm of this immigration, or representative of the flow of immigration through other ports of entry in the early nineteenth century, is difficult to say. Government statistics on immigration are available only from 1820 and are in any case unreliable, failing even to draw a distinction between passengers and immigrants until 1856. German and Irish immigrants—a growing number of the latter from the south of Ireland—outnumbered all other nationalities represented in the baggage lists, but their proportion in the total immigration, as a result of these deficiencies, cannot now be determined. How many immigrants reached port despite the Embargo and the British blockade, how many transferred to coastal vessels or arrived, uncounted, in ordinary packet ships, we cannot know with any certainty. The records are mute. The Philadelphia baggage lists alone give proof of a continuous if irregular flow of immigration during this period, and they are the only records which exist in sufficient quantity to help us in our study of this immigration. It cannot be claimed that they are a true picture, however, merely the largest continuous picture available.

———————

The original baggage lists for the years 1800 to 1819 and for scattered dates beyond are housed today in the Temple University–Balch Institute Center for Immigration Research in Philadelphia. (For more on the Center for Immigration Research see chapter 3.) Baggage lists of a later date, extending well into the century, are in the custody of the National Archives in Washington (Record Group 36). The 1800-1819 lists, included in the National Archives' microfilm publication of the Philadelphia Customs Passenger Lists (M425), have been transcribed in their entirety and published in a reconstituted format as *Passenger Arrivals at the Port of Philadelphia 1800-1819,* ed. Michael Tepper, transcr. Elizabeth P. Bentley (Baltimore: Genealogical Publishing Company, 1986). There are a handful of lists dated October to December 1799 which were not included in the microfilm publication of the Philadelphia baggage lists. They, too, are in the custody of the National Archives, Record Group 36, and are found amongst a group of inward-bound cargo manifests dated 1789-99.

NOTES

1. Passenger arrivals noted in *The Shamrock* have been transcribed and published in Donald M. Schlegel, *Passengers from Ireland: Lists of Passengers Arriving at American Ports Between 1811 and 1817* (Baltimore: Genealogical Publishing Company, 1980). Records of foreign arrivals at the port of Philadelphia, 1727-1808, are discussed in chapter 1.

2. "Passenger Arrivals at Salem and Beverly, Mass., 1798 1800," *New England Historical and Genealogical Register* 106 (1952): 204.

3. The figure representing the total number of ship lists for this period is derived from an aggregation of the ship lists given in *National Archives Microfilm Publications Pamphlet Describing M425; Passenger Lists of Vessels Arriving at Philadelphia 1800-1882* (Washington, D.C.: National Archives and Records Service, 1971).

CUSTOMS PASSENGER LISTS

BACKGROUND

In December of 1818 Representative Thomas Newton of Virginia, the chairman of the influential Committee on Commerce and Manufactures, addressed the House on the necessity of a bill to regulate passenger ships entering American ports from abroad. Of the five thousand passengers who sailed from Antwerp for the United States the previous year, he reported, no fewer than one thousand died before reaching their port of destination. On one ship setting out from a European port, more than 700 of the 1,267 persons aboard perished from a variety of evils associated with "ship fever," a pestilence bred by conditions in the crowded steerage decks. On most emigrant vessels, he argued, provisions, sanitation, and ventilation were so abominable that unless there was some improvement in conditions, many others could be expected to perish. And with immigration mounting, with accounts of fresh horrors reported almost daily, a remedy had to be found at once.

To its credit, Congress acted swiftly. Less than three months later, on 2 March 1819, it enacted legislation which was designed for the first time to regulate the conveyance of passengers in ships and vessels embarking from foreign ports. The object of the legislation was to alleviate overcrowding—to be achieved, in part, by fixing the limit of two passengers for every five tons of a ship's register. In theory, this would restrict the number of passengers to the convenience which the ships afforded. Well-intentioned as this law was, however, it proved to be only marginally effective. In the view of the authors of the authoritative *Report of the Immigration Commission* on immigration legislation, in fact, its benefits were questionable. "Just how much good resulted from its operation and what real benefits it conferred on the emigrant passenger are matters of doubt. . . . By the limiting of the number of passengers according to the total tonnage of the ship rather than according to the tonnage capacity of the steerage, the emigrant was left as badly off in the matter of space as before."[1] But whatever else its shortcomings—and there were notable deficiencies in matters relating to provisions and cargo space—the 1819 law was a necessary first step toward regulation. If little good resulted immediately, at least the first administrative controls on immigration were in place.

More important for our purposes, the provision of the act fixing the limit of two passengers for every five tons of a ship's register turned out to be the basis for an enumeration or listing of all ships' passengers— cabin and steerage, immigrants and non-immigrants—and thus the mechanism for an epic documentation. The records resulting from this documentation we now refer to as Customs Passenger Lists. Throughout the century—until 1891 at the port of Baltimore, 1897 at the port of New York, 1899 at Boston and Philadelphia, and 1902 at the port of New Orleans—Customs Passenger Lists furnish proof of the arrival in the United States of nearly twenty million persons. Although thousands of the passengers enrolled in these lists were neither immigrants nor alien passengers, and countless thousands of newcomers migrated overland from Canada and Mexico and therefore don't appear in the records at all, Customs Passenger Lists remain the primary source of arrival data for the vast majority of immigrants to the United States in the nineteenth century. With the single exception of federal census records they are the largest, the most continuous, and the most uniform body of records of the entire century.

By the middle of the century new laws were enacted which modified or superseded various provisions of the 1819 act, in some cases providing for specific allocations of space for each passenger or changing the proportions to one passenger for every two tons of register, while in other cases demanding specific procedures for ventilation and sanitation or requiring increased rations. But the act of 1819, called *An Act to Regulate Passenger Ships and Vessels* (3 Stat. 488), continued to be

Passengers on the *Ann* and the *Bonny Bess* (arrived Virginia 1623) who subscribed to the oaths of supremacy and allegiance. Manuscript in "Minutes of the Council and General Court, 1622-1629," in the Thomas Jefferson Papers, Library of Congress. (See p. 16.)

Cover page of Thomas Mayhew's register of persons leaving England to "passe into forraigne partes," 1637. (Public Record Office, London.)

Signers of the oath of abjuration, September 20, 1764, administered in Philadelphia to "foreigners" imported on the ship *Sarah*. From Strassburger and Hinke's *Pennsylvania German Pioneers,* vol. 2 (1934). Original in Pennsylvania State Archives, Harrisburg.

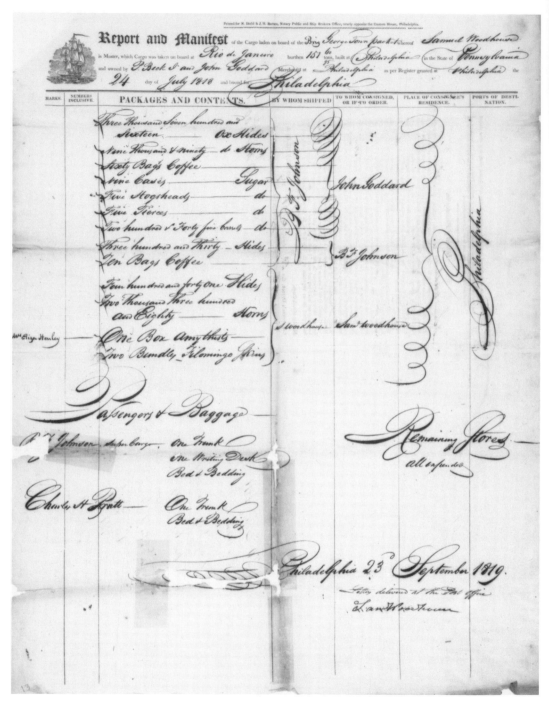

A "baggage list" of the ship *Georgetown Packet,* arrived Philadelphia September 23, 1819. (Courtesy Temple University-Balch Institute Center for Immigration Research.)

Liste of Passengers of the Bremer Ship Johannes
D. von Fritzen Master Bound for Baltimore.

Names	Where from	Whither	Male	Female	Occupation	Age
in the Cabin						
Auguste Pertzch	Querfurt	Baltimore		1		28
Marie do	do	do		1		5
Margaretha do	do	do		1		2
Bertha Kroppenstedt	Halle a/S	do		1		26
Margaretha Meyer	Pardewisch	do		1		20
Carl Nölle	Hille	do	1		Apothecary	47
Jenny do	do	do		1		37
Christoph Bötticher	Mühlhausen	St. Louis	1		Merchant	20
in the second Cabin on Deck						
Bernhardt Budike	Cincinnati	Cincinnati	1		Smith	31
Joseph Pohlmeyer	do	do	1		Merchant	33
Bertha Nölle	Hille	Baltimore		1		17
Emma do	do	do		1		15
Carl do	do	do	1			13
Adelheid do	do	do		1		11
Ottilie do	do	do		1		9
Ida do	do	do		1		3
Valentin Pfaendner	Klein Hul	Pittsburg	1		Farmer	14
Bernhard Kohlmeyer	Damme	Cincinnati	1		do	28
Heinrich Strathmann	Fichtep	do	1		do	24
Johann do	do	do	1		do	20
Johann Rose	Hildritt	Baltimore	1		Buchbinder	36
Conrad Poss	Frutenstoff	do	1		Farmer	43
Gottlob Meyer	Suhl	do	1		Shoemaker	28
Caroline do	do	do		1		23
Heinrich Friedrich	Mingersdorf	do	1		Buchbinder	20
Lorenz Herbst	Butzfeld	do	1		Farmer	40
Theodor Meinike	Sophienthal	do	1		Shoemaker	30
Johannis Hilsinger	Mittelgrimm	Cincinnati	1		Farmer	39
Regine Kluth	Bichenrinde	Galena		1		24
Wilhelm Bordner	Bionde	Cincinnati	1		Farmer	18
Friedrich Nebos	do	do	1		Smith	17
Heinrich do	do	do	1			15
Georg Hösch	Gross Hul	Pittsburg	1		Farmer	22

A Baltimore "City List" of passengers on the ship *Johannes,* arrived May 5, 1854. (Courtesy Baltimore City Archives.)

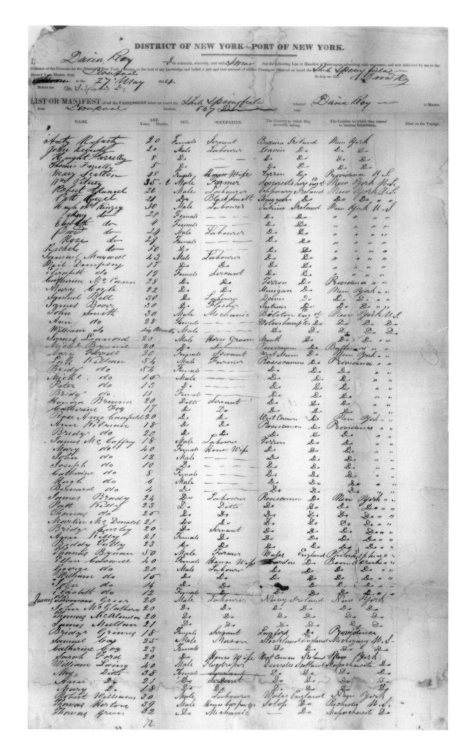

A Customs Passenger List of the ship *Springfeila* (sic), arrived New York May 27, 1844. (Courtesy Temple University-Balch Institute Center for Immigration Research.)

An Immigration Passenger List of the ship *Manilla*, arrived New Orleans February 14, 1903. (National Archives Record Group 85.)

LIST OR MANIFEST OF ALIEN IMMIGRANTS FOR THE COMMISSIONER OF IMMIGRATION

Required by the regulations of the Secretary of the Treasury of the United States, under Act of Congress approved March 3, 1893, to be delivered to the Commissioner of Immigration by the Commanding officer or agent having such passengers on board upon arrival at a port in the United States.

S.S. _Manilla_ sailing from _Palermo_ _____, 19_____

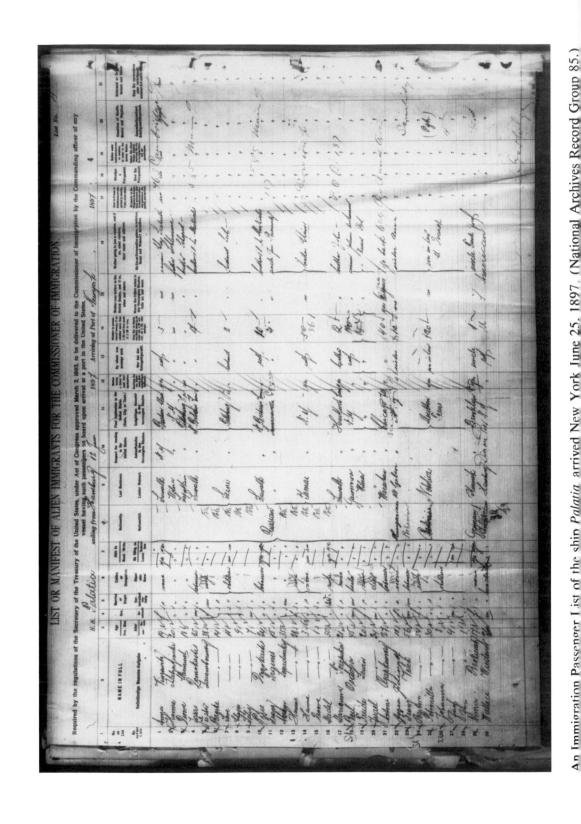

An Immigration Passenger List of the ship *Palatia* arrived New York June 25, 1897. (National Archives Record Group 85.)

the inspiration for almost all subsequent legislation, and changes brought about by later enactments tended only to reinforce the humanitarian intent of the original statute.

Under the 1819 act masters of vessels arriving at American ports from abroad were required to submit a list or manifest of all passengers to the collector of the customs district in which the ship arrived, designating, in particular, "the age, sex, and occupation of the said passengers, respectively, the country to which they severally belong, and that of which it is their intention to become inhabitants" (section 4). In addition, the customs collectors were required to deliver, "quarter yearly," copies of the passenger lists to the Secretary of State, by whom statements were to be laid before Congress at every session. The original passenger lists and the copies and quarterly abstracts prepared by the customs collectors, as well as transcripts of the quarterly returns developed by the State Department, make up, in the aggregate, the body of records known as Customs Passenger Lists (classified by the National Archives under Records of the U.S. Customs Service, Record Group 36).

The original lists were kept under the authority of the collectors of customs at the various ports of entry or customs districts, while copies of the lists, as well as abstracts, or consolidated quarterly reports, were maintained by the State Department, presumably until 1874, when an act of Congress repealed the provision of the 1819 statute requiring customs collectors to send copies of the passenger lists to the Secretary of State and directed instead that they send only statistical reports on passenger arrivals to the Secretary of the Treasury. All the lists— originals, copies, and abstracts, as well as the transcripts developed on the initiative of the State Department—were eventually acquired by the National Archives in Washington, D.C., where they were sorted and arranged by port, date, and ship. In the spring of 1977, after their preservation had been assured by placing them on microfilm, the lists for the five major ports of entry—Boston, New York, Philadelphia, Baltimore, and New Orleans—were transferred to the Temple University–Balch Institute Center for Immigration Research in Philadelphia (not the State Department Transcripts, however, nor any lists for the smaller ports of entry). For its part, the Center for Immigration Research has a mandate to furnish the Archives eventually with an index to the New York Customs Passenger Lists for the fifty years from 1847 to June 1897, as yet the greatest stumbling block in immigration research. At the present time, owing to limited facilities, the Center is not open to the general public.

CHARACTERISTICS AND LIMITATIONS

As far as is known all extant Customs Passenger Lists have been accessioned by the National Archives, and just about all have been microfilmed. This includes the lists for the five major ports of entry as well as a number of lesser ports on the Atlantic and the Gulf. With the exception of some recently discovered lists for San Francisco (1903-18) and Port Townsend and Tacoma, Washington (1894-1909)—unusually late for Customs Passenger Lists—lists for Pacific Coast ports do not appear to be extant. (The earlier Customs Passenger Lists for San Francisco were destroyed by fires in 1851 and 1940; in fact, all lists of passengers arriving at San Francisco were thought to have been destroyed until the recent dramatic discovery of a trove of later Immigration Passenger Lists for San Francisco and various other Pacific and Gulf Coast ports, as well as the two series of Customs Passenger Lists noted above—but see chapter 4.) In no case do original passenger lists run in an uninterrupted sequence right up to the end of the century. Date spans at any one port conceal numerous gaps in the records, with coverage varying quite considerably from one port to another. Boston, for instance, has no original lists dated earlier than 1883.

Fortunately, copies and abstracts of the passenger lists prepared by the customs collectors are extant for most ports for various years from 1820 to 1874 and are used with surprisingly effective results to fill in gaps in the original passenger lists. From the very beginning, when the National Archives took on the project of microfilming the Customs Passenger Lists, they carefully substituted copies and abstracts for missing or illegible originals, giving each port the most complete coverage possible. They also included cargo manifests for the port of Philadelphia, 1800-1819 (the Philadelphia "baggage lists"), and "City

Lists," 1833-66, for the port of Baltimore, neither of which, technically, falls under the classification of Customs Passenger Lists. Under the same ambitious program, the Archives microfilmed special indexes to the lists, many of which had been prepared by the Work Projects Administration (WPA) in the 1930s. (For a listing of the indexes on microfilm see Table 1.)

Despite their availability on microfilm (and despite the indexes), systematic access to the data in the lists often eludes us. Quite apart from the difficulties one encounters in reading old handwriting—and the lists are written in various hands with great originality of style, spelling, and punctuation—the lists themselves are cumbersome and awkward to use, even on microfilm. There are thousands of lists, after all, and they are arranged by port of entry, then according to the date or quarter date of the ship's arrival, then by ship, and finally, without order, by passengers' names. The indexes—which are the usual means of access to such records—might be supposed to hold the key, but some of the most important indexes are incomplete. They are also arranged in different ways, some in alphabetical order by passengers' surnames, some by soundex (first letter of surname followed by numerical codes representing letters of the same or similar sound but different spellings); they might contain all the information needed concerning the arrival of a passenger or just enough to point the researcher in the direction of the passenger lists. All are subject to copying errors, of course, and must be used with care. (Although not an infallible method, records of individual passengers can generally be located through existing indexes providing the port of arrival and the approximate date of arrival are known.)

By far the most serious limitation of Customs Passenger Lists is the lack of a complete index to passengers disembarking at the port of New York. Although the WPA compiled indexes to passengers arriving at Baltimore (1820-97), Boston (1848-91), New Orleans (1853-99), and Philadelphia (1800-1906), they failed to carry the New York index beyond 1846, cutting it off the very year that saw the beginning of mass migration from Ireland. We can only conclude that they were defeated by the sheer magnitude of the records after 1846 and were forced to abandon the attempt. In any case, the WPA index to passenger arrivals at the port of New York stops dead at the end of 1846 (it is an index to *copies* of the lists at that), and until June of 1897, a full fifty years later, there is no index to passenger arrivals at this key port of entry. This is a very serious impediment to research, of course, but in spite of it records of individual passengers can often be located if either the name of the vessel or the exact date of arrival is known. To explain how this works we can do no better than to quote the *Guide to Genealogical Research in the National Archives:*

> If the name of the port of entry and the approximate arrival date are known, *it may be possible to determine the exact date and the name of the vessel from records of vessel entrances maintained at the ports* [my italics]. These records, which are in Record Group 36, show the name of each vessel, its captain, the port of embarkation, and the date of arrival. For some ports there are two series, one with entries arranged alphabetically by name of vessel, and the other with entries arranged chronologically. If, in addition to the port of entry and approximate date of arrival, the port of embarkation is known, the search for the name of the vessel and the exact date may be facilitated. For example, if a passenger embarked from Stockholm for New York in a year in which 500 passenger vessels arrived in New York, the search could be narrowed to the relatively few passenger lists for vessels sailing from Stockholm.[2]

Another strategy, although it will almost certainly be more successful with the later Immigration Passenger Lists, is to use the *Morton Allan Directory of European Passenger Steamship Arrivals* (1931; reprint, Baltimore: Genealogical Publishing Company, 1979). By year and by steamship company—for New York from 1890 to 1930, and for Philadelphia, Boston, and Baltimore from 1904 to 1926—the *Morton Allan Directory* lists the name of the vessel, the exact date of its arrival, and its European port of embarkation. Thus, if the port of entry and the approximate arrival date are known, it *may* be possible, by consulting the *Directory,* to determine the name of the passenger line and the name of the vessel. If the port of embarkation is known, it may be possible to narrow the search even further. And if the name of the vessel and the name of the line are known, it may be possible to determine the exact date of arrival, all of which brings the passenger manifest closer to retrieval.

Besides the *Morton Allan Directory*, which was compiled from records of the steamship lines, a new work listing passenger ships arriving at the port of New York from 1820 to 1850 might also be useful in tracking down specific passenger lists. Based on official lists of vessel entrances at the port of New York as well as Customs Passenger Lists, and intended as the first in a series of volumes which will document vessel arrivals at the port of New York for the whole period from 1820 to 1897, *Passenger Ships Arriving in New York Harbor (1820-1850)*, ed. Bradley W. Steuart (Bountiful, Utah: Precision Indexing, 1991), lists vessel entrances in alphabetical order by name of ship and chronologically by date of arrival, supplying, among other useful bits of information, the ship manifest number, the National Archives microfilm roll number, and the name of the port of embarkation, and giving not only the name of the port, or ports, at which each ship docked enroute to New York, but the order in which each port was visited.

Later volumes in this series will of course be more useful in circumventing the lacunae of the 1847-97 period, but it is interesting to note that this projected series is actually the spearhead of a larger program by Precision Indexing to compile a complete index of passengers arriving at the port of New York from 1847 to 1897. That the project depends on volunteer labor is not to diminish it in any way but merely to emphasize again the problems of scale. Indeed, since the demise of the old WPA there have been numerous attempts to index the post-1847 New York passenger arrival records, but for a variety of reasons, not least a lack of resources, all of them have foundered. Even an attempt by the Genealogical Publishing Company of Baltimore to publish Customs Passenger Lists on a port by port basis, under the aegis of its Passenger Arrivals program, was abandoned after the publication of only two volumes of passenger lists, one for Baltimore, one for Philadelphia (q.v.). In the meantime, complying with its agreement with the National Archives, the Center for Immigration Research, funded partly by its massive publications program (see pp. 78-81), continues to expand its giant data base and may yet be first past the post in the New York sweepstakes.

ORIGINAL LISTS

The original passenger lists—the captains' lists—were prepared on board ship and deposited with the collector of customs when the ship reached port. These lists—printed forms for which were provided—contain the following information: the name of the customs district and port, a statement sworn to and signed by the master certifying that the passenger list is "a just and true account," the name of the ship, the name of the port of embarkation, the date of the ship's arrival, and an estimate of the ship's tonnage, and, for each passenger, his name, age, sex, and occupation, the name of the country to which he belonged, the name of the country of which he intended becoming an inhabitant, and, if he died en route, the date or circumstances of his death. It must be emphasized that until quite late in the century—after 1882, for the most part, when new immigration laws required substantially different data of each passenger—this is the only information provided on passengers in the Customs Passenger Lists.

Original lists exist for the five major ports of entry and a handful of lesser ports on the Atlantic Coast and the Gulf of Mexico, and run irregularly from 1820 to the end of the century. Portions of years, whole years, and entire blocks of years are missing from the records, Boston and Baltimore being especially unfortunate in this regard. But gaps and irregularities in such records are not unexpected. It's unlikely, after all, that they were preserved under ideal conditions in the various customs houses, and over the years some of them may have been purposely destroyed (copies or abstracts, remember, had been sent in to the State Department, at least until 1874). Other lists were almost certainly lost through negligence or attrition. Many were destroyed by fire. Besides the San Francisco lists, the original lists of passengers arriving at Boston prior to 1883 were destroyed this way, and the early Baltimore lists are reported to have been destroyed by a fire in 1897. Other lists, possibly, were lost or misplaced as a result of changes in departmental jurisdiction. Some we can be sure were deliberately disposed of, since further use for them wasn't anticipated, while still others may yet be in local repositories, misfiled, forgotten, or undetected amidst an accumulation of other documents. This is precisely what happened with a group of about forty-five passenger lists of vessels entering the port of Baltimore in 1839. These lists—City Lists, it is presumed—had been misfiled by Historical Records Survey personnel during one of their inventory sweeps, and were discovered in the Baltimore City Archives in the early 1980s, forty years later! Even now their whereabouts may be unknown to the National Archives.

COPIES AND ABSTRACTS

In accordance with a provision of the act of 2 March 1819, copies and abstracts of the original lists were prepared by the collectors of customs and sent once each quarter to the Secretary of State, whose reports, compiled from the quarterly returns and published between 1820 and 1870 as Congressional documents, indicate by port of arrival the number of passengers, their nationality and occupation, and sometimes their age and sex. (Only reports for the first three quarters of 1820 contain the names of passengers.) Copies of the original passenger lists usually specify the name of the vessel, the name of the port of embarkation, the name of the port of arrival, and sometimes the name of the master and the date of arrival. Abstracts of the original lists, on the other hand, usually indicate the name of the customs district or port, the quarter year of arrival (generally a quarter ending date), and sometimes the name of the port of embarkation. (While there are exceptions, the name of the vessel is generally not given in the abstracts.) In all other details copies and abstracts agree with the original lists, except that sometimes passengers' given names are shortened to initials.

All extant copies and abstracts were given to the National Archives where, as substitutes for missing or illegible originals, they have proved indispensable in the reconstruction of the passenger arrival records. They are available—with gaps themselves—for the following years: for the port of Baltimore, from 1820 to 1869 (gaps); for Boston, from 1820 to 1874 (gaps); for New Orleans, from 1820 to 1875; for New York, from 1820 to 1874; and for Philadelphia, from 1820 to 1854. For the smaller ports of entry there are decidedly more copies extant than abstracts. For a complete list of those on microfilm see Table 1.

Boston lists for the period from 1820 to 1874 are copies of original lists, and, with the exception of lists transcribed by the State Department for quarter-year periods between 1820 and 1827, they are the only federal passenger lists available for the port of Boston before 1883. The Baltimore lists for the period from 1820 to 1869, on the other hand, are quarterly abstracts of original lists, and are supplementary to both the original lists and the City Lists and actually comprise a separate microfilm publication.

There are two partially complete alphabetical card indexes to the copies and abstracts of passenger lists, one to passengers arriving at the port of New York, 1820-46 (noted above), the other an index to passengers arriving at other Atlantic and Gulf Coast ports, 1820-74, called *A Supplemental Index to Passenger Lists of Vessels Arriving at Atlantic and Gulf Coast Ports (Excluding New York), 1820-1874* (National Archives microfilm publication M334). These also serve as indexes to some of the original passenger lists as well as to certain volumes of State Department Transcripts.

STATE DEPARTMENT TRANSCRIPTS

Also included under the heading of Customs Passenger Lists are the State Department Transcripts of lists of passengers arriving at Atlantic and Gulf Coast ports between 1819 and 1832. The transcripts, originally in nine volumes (Volume 2 is now missing), were prepared in the office of the Secretary of State from the copies of lists and quarterly abstracts received from the collectors of customs. Although the 1819 statute made no mention of a compilation, but merely required the Secretary of State to submit periodic "statements" to Congress, it is believed the transcripts were prepared to facilitate publication of the lists, and in fact the first volume of the transcripts and a small part of the missing second volume were published in 1821 by order of the Senate under the title *Letter from the Secretary of State, with a Transcript of the List of Passengers Who Arrived in the United States from 1st October, 1819, to the 30th September, 1820* (16th Cong., 2d sess., S. Doc. 118, serial 45; reprint (under the title *Passenger Arrivals 1819-1820*), Baltimore: Genealogical Publishing Company, 1971). The last eighteen pages of this work contain the final entries for the quarter year ending 30 September which no doubt appeared at the beginning of the missing volume of transcripts. The nearly 600 passengers who are named, all but a handful of whom are recorded as having arrived at the port of New York, can thus be found in the published work but not in the extant transcripts. The remaining State Department Transcripts, for whatever reason, were left unpublished. Recently, after nearly 150 years, the third volume and a part of the fourth were published, appearing under the title *Passengers Who Arrived in the United States, September 1821–December 1823* (Baltimore: Magna Carta Book Company, 1969), but no further volumes have appeared.

For reasons that can only be surmised, the State Department Transcripts aren't complete for the period 1819-32—not even counting the missing volume. In fact, the sequence of coverage is interrupted at several points, with gaps of quarters and whole years for greater and lesser ports alike. (Technically, there aren't any gaps in the transcripts for the year 1819, even though only twenty-nine passengers—twelve of them shipwrecked seamen—are recorded as arriving that year, for official depositions weren't actually required until January 1, 1820.) For the port of Baltimore the transcripts comprise lists of passengers arriving during the years 1820, 1822-27, and 1829; for Boston, New Orleans, and New York, 1820-27; and for Philadelphia, 1820-22, 1824-27, and 1829. Despite gaps and omissions, and even errors in transcription—which have been noted by officials at the National Archives—the State Department Transcripts contain some records that are not otherwise known, those of New York arrivals in the second quarter of 1820, for instance.

The transcripts regularly list the passengers by port or customs district, then by quarter year of arrival, and thereunder by name, a typical entry indicating the passenger's age, sex, and occupation, and the name of the country to which he belonged and the country of which he intended becoming an inhabitant, together with the name of the ship on which he arrived and the name of its master—essentially a duplication of the quarterly abstracts.

Entries in Volumes 5, 8, and 9 have been indexed as part of *A Supplemental Index to Passenger Lists of Vessels Arriving at Atlantic and Gulf Coast Ports (Excluding New York), 1820-1874* (M334). Volume 1 and a small portion of the missing second volume, and Volume 3 and a part of Volume 4, have been indexed in their published forms (there is also a manuscript index to Volume 1 in the National Archives Library), leaving only Volumes 4 (partially), 6, and 7 without an index.

There is apparently some doubt about the classification of the transcripts as Customs Passenger Lists, and the fact is they do not enjoy the legitimacy conferred on the other passenger arrival records by the act of 1819. What is more, they were not included by the National Archives in the microfilm publication of the Customs Passenger Lists. However, it is not our concern to argue their classification one way or the other. What is absolutely clear is that omissions and discrepancies in the primary record sources make them indispensable, and since they were compiled at an early date, when the returns were crisp and unblemished, the ink fresh and the style of handwriting familiar, they are invaluable as an alternative reading of the quarterly returns.

A View of the Records at the Principal Ports of Entry

Most immigrants in the nineteenth century landed at the ports of Boston, New York, Philadelphia, Baltimore, or New Orleans, so records deposited at these ports are of paramount interest to the researcher. Given below, then, as a means of introduction and orientation, are highlights of the existing records and indexes for these five principal ports of entry. (For a listing of the records and indexes available for other ports of entry on the Atlantic and the Gulf see Table 1.)

Boston

As mentioned previously, all original Customs Passenger Lists for Boston dated earlier than 1883 were destroyed by a fire, leaving the port almost destitute of records. Nevertheless, with State Department Transcripts from 1820 to 1827 (with some gaps), and copies of original lists from 1820 to 1874 (also with gaps), there is only a ten-year hiatus in the federal passenger records. By chance, a Massachusetts alien passenger act of 1848 which required a bond of indemnity or the payment of $2.00 for each passenger landed from abroad, also required that passenger lists be kept, specifying names, ages, occupations, birthplaces, dates of arrival, and names of vessels. (A similar law was enacted in 1837, indemnifying local jurisdictions against alien passengers who might become public charges, but no lists were called for.) The "State Lists," extending from 1848 to 1891, not only bridge the ten-year gap from 1874 to 1883 in the Customs Passenger Lists but also overlap the *copies* (1848-74) and the extant *originals* (1883-99), thereby providing an added measure of cover. In addition, in Record Group 36 in the National Archives, there are "journals of and alphabetical indexes to vessel entrances, which also serve as finding aids to names of vessels and dates of arrival for most of the period 1874-91; and eight volumes of letters received by the Boston collector of customs relating to quarantine and immigration, 1884-99, in which there are names of passengers" (quoted from *National Archives Microfilm Publications Pamphlet Accompanying M277: Passenger Lists of Vessels Arriving at Boston 1820-1891* [Washington, D.C.: National Archives and Records Service, 1970], 2). The State Lists are held at the Massachusetts State Archives in Boston and are not available on microfilm at the National Archives except in the form of an index, but see below.

Indexes

There are two indexes to passengers arriving at the port of Boston, both available on microfilm at the National Archives: (1) *A Supplemental Index to Passenger Lists of Vessels Arriving at Atlantic and Gulf Coast Ports (Excluding New York), 1820-1874* (M334), which, though incomplete, is the only finding-aid to Boston passenger lists for the period prior to 1848; and (2) an *Index to Passenger Lists of Vessels Arriving at Boston, 1848-1891* (M265). This is an index to the State Lists. The original alphabetical card index prepared by the WPA is in the Massachusetts State Archives.

Published Lists

A curious and little-known publication—an outgrowth of the 1848 alien passenger act—concerns passengers who were placed in public care between 1847 and 1851. A *List of Alien Passengers Bonded from January 1, 1847 to January 1, 1851, for the Use of the Overseers of the Poor in the Commonwealth* (1851; reprint, Baltimore: Genealogical Publishing Company, 1971) is a loosely alphabetized list of about 5,000 paupers (mostly Irish) who entered the Commonwealth and went immediately onto public charity. While only a small percentage of the 100,000 passengers known to have arrived in Boston during the period 1847-51 are mentioned, it is nonetheless a revealing document, and reflects another melancholy aspect of the tragedy unfolding in Ireland at that time.

New York

The total number of immigrants arriving at the port of New York climbed from a few thousand in 1820 to a few hundred thousand a year by the 1880s and 1890s, an aggregate of about fifteen million for the whole period from 1820 to 1900, if we allow for the fact that government statistics make no distinction between passengers and immigrants until 1856, or between alien passengers and immigrants until 1868. Dwarfing the records of all other ports, New York's Customs Passenger Lists are largely complete from 1820 to June 17, 1897 and run in a surprisingly consistent pattern. Classified as part of National Archives Record Group 36, Records of the U.S. Customs Service, they consist of original passenger lists, 1820-97, copies of the lists, 1820-74, and State Department Transcripts, 1820-27. The Archives' microfilm publication of the original lists, M237 (675 rolls), includes a large number of copies for the period 1820-74 which were inserted in place of missing or illegible originals. Supplementary passenger lists, similar to those for other major ports of entry, are not known to exist for New York. Nevertheless, New York laws of 1819, 1824, and 1849 called for the keeping of arrival records of one description or another, and although investigations have so far failed to bring any to light, it's highly probable, as was the recent experience at the Baltimore City Archives, that some local records will eventually turn up.

Also in Record Group 36 are journals of and alphabetical indexes to vessel entrances at the port of New York which serve as finding aids to names of vessels and dates of arrival for most of the period from 1820 to 1897. Owing in part to their value as finding aids, the National Archives has microfilmed the lot, publishing them as *Registers of*

Vessels Arriving at the Port of New York from Foreign Ports, 1789-1919 (M1066). The registers and indexes in this micropublication are arranged in two series. The volumes that make up the first series, dated August 5, 1789–December 30, 1899, in the words of a National Archives catalogue, "originally were maintained by the offices of the collector, naval officer, and surveyor of the Port of New York. Because the records were created by these offices for different purposes, the volumes vary in internal arrangement, dates covered, and information recorded. The volumes have been combined as a single series because they all record the arrival of vessels from foreign ports and, as such, provide the most complete record available of these vessel arrivals at New York." [3] The second series, dated January 3, 1860–December 31, 1919, is an index to vessel arrivals, the volumes arranged alphabetically by the name of the vessel and chronologically thereunder. Few passengers are named in these registers, of course, but as already mentioned they do have value as finding aids; for the salient fact about New York is that there is no index to passenger arrivals for the entire period from 1847 to June 1897, and therefore no systematic means of access to the records of the several million immigrants who disembarked at the great depots of Castle Garden and Ellis Island—not until the middle of 1897, at any rate. While there are various methods for getting round this problem, starting with knowing the exact name of the ship or its date of arrival—hence the importance of the journals and indexes to vessel entrances, but see the discussion on page 68—the fact remains that there is no quick remedy and no assurance that the record sought will ever be found. When the singular nature of the information stored in these records is taken into account (after 1882, for instance, there is information on country of citizenship, native country, and destination in the U.S.; after 1893 last place of residence, marital status, and if going to join a relative, his name and address), the want of an index becomes acute.

Indexes

The lack of an index for 1847-97 is unfortunate, and therefore the researcher will appreciate the growing number of index substitutes discussed below under the heading "Published Lists." There is also some consolation in the fact that the National Archives has an index to passenger arrival records for the quarter-century immediately preceding—

Index to Passenger Lists of Vessels Arriving at New York, 1820-1846 (M261). Just one caveat, however. This is an alphabetical card index to copies of the original passenger lists rather than an index to the original lists themselves. Since it is unlikely that there were extant copies of all original lists when the WPA undertook the indexing project in the mid-1930s, it is probable that some passenger lists were left out.

Published Lists

In place of an index there are several publications that deal with specific immigrant groups arriving at New York at selected time periods —all based on Customs Passenger Lists. The largest of these by far is *Germans to America: Lists of Passengers Arriving at U.S. Ports,* ed. Ira A. Glazier and P. William Filby (Wilmington, Del.: Scholarly Resources, Inc., 1988-). When completed, this mammoth project (of which thirty volumes have been published so far) will span the years 1850 to 1892 and reach fifty volumes, naming perhaps 4.5 million German surname immigrants, or a very substantial proportion of the names on the heretofore unindexed manifests. Listing either German surname immigrants or those who declared themselves to be of German origin, this work casts both a wider and a shallower net than might at first be supposed—wider in that it includes those who originated from areas outside the as yet undefined borders of Germany; shallower in that it arbitrarily limits inclusion to individuals arriving in ships carrying at least 80 percent German passengers (the requirement for inclusion in the first nine volumes) or to any and all passengers "calling themselves Germans" (the requirement in all subsequent volumes). Above all there is the question of who is or is not German, in essence the tedious ethnic versus national origin question, but this isn't an issue that can be resolved definitively or even satisfactorily in a work of this kind; it can merely be handled, and the method chosen has enabled the compilers to trawl widely if imperfectly in the Customs Passenger Lists, offering the researcher at least one promising route of access to the New York arrival records (and to records of other ports of entry as well). To balance the ledger it must be said that doubts have been raised about the criteria for inclusion and about the 'compilers' use of original records over copies, the originals being held by the Center for Immigration

Research, chief architects of the project, with similar doubts being raised about *The Famine Immigrants* (q.v.).[4]

Another effort of the Temple-Balch Center for Immigration Research, and next in scale (for the moment), is *The Famine Immigrants: Lists of Irish Immigrants Arriving at the Port of New York, 1846-1851*, ed. Ira A. Glazier and Michael Tepper, 7 vols. (Baltimore: Genealogical Publishing Company, 1983-86). Transcribed from original records in the custody of the Center, this work contains passenger lists which identify more than a half-million immigrants who fled the Potato Famine and took part in the epic movement that helped pave the way for the mass migrations of the second half of the nineteenth century. (Brian Mitchell's recently published *Irish Passenger Lists 1847-1871: Lists of Passengers Sailing from Londonderry to America on Ships of the J. & J. Cooke Line and the McCorkell Line* [Baltimore: Genealogical Publishing Company, 1988] does something of this in reverse, as it identifies emigrants from records kept by passenger lines at the port of departure.) The Center did not always succeed in stripping out non-Irish passengers from the lists, however, and the researcher will be amused to find that a few Cornish and Welsh passenger lists (and some others) have been incorporated inter alia; at the same time, since it was not always possible to differentiate between the Irish and non-Irish passengers who sailed from English ports and who claimed Great Britain as their country of allegiance (which was the case with many of the Irish), an indeterminate number of other non-Irish passengers are necessarily included in the work. Yet on balance, apart from the fact that it does not make use of the microfilmed version of the passenger lists, *The Famine Immigrants* seems to have benefitted from a policy of inclusion rather than exclusion.

Broader in scope than *The Famine Immigrants*, though not so large a work, is *Dutch Immigrants in U.S. Ship Passenger Manifests 1820-1880*, ed. Robert P. Swierenga, 2 vols. (Wilmington, Del.: Scholarly Resources, Inc., 1983). An exhaustive listing of Dutch immigrants arriving at New York (and other ports as well), this outsize publication—oblong, in imitation of the manifests—was painstakingly developed from an examination of 100,000 passenger lists—in itself an heroic feat and unmatched by any other work to date. In a similar vein, Nils William Olsson's *Swedish Passenger Arrivals in New York, 1820-*

1850 (Chicago: Swedish Pioneer Historical Society, 1967), based on a study of 33,000 manifests, is an extraction of data on Swedish immigrants—but only up to mid-century. A companion volume, *Swedish Passenger Arrivals in U.S. Ports 1820-1850 (Except New York)* (Saint Paul, Minn.: North Central Publishing, 1979), contains additions and corrections to the New York volume.

Somewhat narrower in approach, but with a unique refinement, is *German Immigrants: Lists of Passengers Bound from Bremen to New York* [vol. 1], *1847-1854*; [vol. 2], *1855-1862*; [vol. 3], *1863-1867*; [vol. 4], *1868-1871*, ed. Gary J. Zimmerman and Marion Wolfert (Baltimore: Genealogical Publishing Company, 1985-93). The refinement has to do with the fact that the 130,000 immigrants listed are those for whom a specific place of origin is recorded—thought by the compilers to represent twenty-one percent of the total number of Germans arriving at the port of New York during the period concerned. Covering approximately the same time period, and also starting with the crucial year 1847, Volume 4 of Leo Baca's *Czech Immigration Passenger Lists* (Richardson, Tex.: the author, 1991) is a listing based on Customs Passenger Lists of over 20,000 Czech arrivals at New York from 1847 to 1869 (earlier volumes in the series cover Czech arrivals at New Orleans and Galveston). More specialized yet is the *Index to Mennonite Immigrants on United States Passenger Lists, 1872-1904*, ed. David A. Haury (North Newton, Kan.: Mennonite Library and Archives, 1986)—a listing of approximately 15,000 Mennonite immigrants— mostly Germans from Russia—who arrived in the last quarter of the century on more than 200 ships, most of which—from Antwerp, Bremen, Hamburg, and Liverpool—put in at New York.

Finally, the Center for Immigration Research, custodians of the Customs Passenger Lists for the five major ports of entry, has under consideration several other publications that could stand as partial substitutes for an index to passenger arrivals in the second half of the nineteenth century. Projects currently in chain include (1) a continuation of Irish passenger arrival lists at the port of New York from 1852, a record of the bitter after-shock of the Great Famine; (2) a multi-volume work covering Russian arrivals at U.S. ports from 1880 to 1892, i.e. from a time just prior to the introduction of the anti-Semitic May laws (which provoked numerous pogroms and precipitated the flight of Russian Jews to the United States and elsewhere) to the year Ellis Island was first opened as an immigrant depot; and (3) a projected ten-volume work entitled *Italians to America, 1880-1899,* the first two volumes of which, covering 1880-87, have already been published. It's expected that this work will contain documentation on the 800,000 Italians who migrated to the United States between 1880 and 1899 in the first major wave of Italian immigration, and that eight of the projected ten volumes will deal with arrivals in New York. (Editors are Ira A. Glazier and P. William Filby, and the publisher is Scholarly Resources of Wilmington, Delaware.) The latest word out of the Center is that the coverage of *Italians to America* and the ongoing *Germans to America* is to be extended to 1914.

Philadelphia

In range and continuity Philadelphia's passenger arrival records surpass those of all other ports of entry. It has nearly continuous records going all the way back to 1727, while its federal passenger lists are among the earliest in existence. In National Archives Record Group 36, Records of the U.S. Customs Service, there are baggage lists from 1800 to 1819 (see chapter 2 for a detailed discussion of these lists), original passenger lists from 1820 to 1899, copies or abstracts of original lists from 1820 to 1854, and State Department Transcripts for the years 1820-22, 1824-27, and 1829. The microfilmed records, National Archives microfilm publication M425, consist of baggage lists from 1800 to 1819 and original passenger lists from 1820 to 1882, with some later baggage lists and copies of original lists inserted as substitutes for missing or illegible originals. In the same record group there are records of vessel arrivals and abstracts of tonnage duties collected at Philadelphia that serve as finding aids to names of vessels and the dates of their arrival for most of the period 1800-82.

Besides the federal passenger lists in the National Archives, a significant body of provincial and early state records of passenger arrivals at Philadelphia can be found at the Pennsylvania State Archives in Harrisburg, specifically, records of "foreign" arrivals, 1727-1808. Virtually unique, these records consist of original "captains' lists" as well as the more comprehensive lists of foreigners who signed the required oaths of allegiance and abjuration (see pp. 17-18). In addition, the Philadelphia City Archives has ships' registers and passenger lists for 1839-43 and 1859-67. These have not been indexed or microfilmed, but the originals can be consulted by the public. It is reported that they include a number of passenger lists not found among the official Customs Passenger Lists, but this hasn't been verified.

Indexes

There are two alphabetical card indexes to passengers arriving at the port of Philadelphia: (1) *Index to Passenger Lists of Vessels Arriving at Philadelphia, 1800-1906* (M360), which contains names from cargo manifests (baggage lists), 1800-19, names from passenger lists, 1820-82, and names from some passenger lists, 1883-1906, which also serves as an index to an important segment of Immigration Passenger Lists; and (2) *A Supplemental Index to Passenger Lists of Vessels Arriving at Atlantic and Gulf Coast Ports (Excluding New York), 1820-1874* (M334). Both indexes are available at the National Archives.

Published Lists

Neither of the two principal works listing passengers arriving at the port of Philadelphia is based on Customs Passenger Lists. Ralph B. Strassburger and William J. Hinke's *Pennsylvania German Pioneers,* a list of approximately 38,000 Germans and Swiss who arrived at Philadelphia between 1727 and 1808, is based on records resulting from legislation designed to regulate the flow of "foreigners" into the province; while *Passenger Arrivals at the Port of Philadelphia 1800-1819,* ed. Michael Tepper, is a transcription of the singular if little-known group of records referred to as baggage lists (see p. 60). Although the baggage lists were included by the National Archives in its microfilm publication of the Philadelphia Customs Passenger Lists, where they comprise the first twenty-nine rolls of film, they are not technically Customs Passenger Lists, owing their origin to a completely unrelated act of Congress. While both books have limitations—the one restricted to foreigners, the other to passengers recorded with baggage—they

nonetheless furnish a continuous picture of immigration into Philadelphia for nearly a full hundred years before the introduction of Customs Passenger Lists.

Baltimore

Original lists for the port of Baltimore are extremely fragmentary,
especially in the early years. Like Boston, many of Baltimore's original
passenger lists were destroyed by fire; like Boston again, gaps in the
original lists are offset by supplementary records—by State Department Transcripts for 1820, 1822-27, and 1829, for instance, and by
quarterly abstracts for the period from 1820 to 1869. The quarterly
abstracts, however, while most helpful in the 1820s and 1830s, are
marred by serious deficiencies: gaps of quarter years are characteristic,
while gaps of entire years exist for 1842, 1844, 1846, 1847, 1851-56,
1864, and 1867. Furthermore, in the National Archives' microfilm
publication of the Baltimore quarterly abstracts, the chronological
arrangement (by quarter-ending date) is sometimes muddled. A few
lists for the last quarter of 1822, for example, are found at the end of
the last quarter of 1829.

Offsetting the lacunae in the federal passenger arrival records, however, are the "City Lists," which run from September 1833 to October
1866. These lists were compiled in compliance with a Maryland law
of 22 March 1833 designed to indemnify the city of Baltimore for
expenses incurred on behalf of immigrants who became public charges.
Although the law only required an enumeration of alien passengers by
name, age, and occupation, the City Lists frequently supply the identical information called for under the act of 1819, and very often
adventitious information, notable especially in lists prepared by masters
of vessels departing from Bremen which designate places of birth,
former places of residence, and places of destination within the United
States, with occasional references to passengers' height and coloring.
In addition, the City Lists contain breakdowns by age groups—mainly
under fives and over fives—as a tax of $1.50 required under the terms
of the Maryland statute was levied only on alien passengers above five
years of age.

Owing to the fragmentary nature of the original passenger lists
(there are in fact less than a dozen original lists prior to September

1833, nine of them cargo manifests) and the unevenness of the quarterly abstracts, the National Archives borrowed the City Lists and used them rather than the abstracts to fill in gaps for the period 1833-66 in its microfilm publication of the original passenger lists (M255), leaving the quarterly abstracts to comprise a separate micropublication (M596). Thus, four categories of passenger arrival records are used in making up a composite record of arrivals at the port of Baltimore: (1) State Department Transcripts (1820, 1822-27, 1829); (2) City Lists (1833-66); (3) quarterly abstracts (1820-69); and (4) original lists (1820-91). As at other ports of entry there are journals and alphabetical indexes to the names and arrival dates of vessels for most of the period 1820-91 (National Archives Record Group 36).

Indexes

There are several indexes to Baltimore passenger arrival records, though there is as yet no index to the quarterly abstracts. Listed below are the indexes that are available, the first three at the National Archives.

1. *A Supplemental Index to Passenger Lists of Vessels Arriving at Atlantic and Gulf Coast Ports (Excluding New York), 1820-1874* (M334). This is an incomplete alphabetical card index to *copies* of passenger lists, which includes entries for vessels arriving at Baltimore up to about 1870. It also serves as an index to some of the original lists as well as to selected volumes of State Department Transcripts.

2. *Index to Passenger Lists of Vessels Arriving at Baltimore, 1820-1897 (Federal Passenger Lists)* (M327). This is a soundex index to lists made in compliance with federal law (M255) and is exclusive of the City Lists. Although M255 comprises both the federal records and the borrowed City Lists, the latter are indexed separately in no. 3 below.

3. *Index to Passenger Lists of Vessels Arriving at Baltimore, 1833-1866 (City Passenger Lists)* (M326). This, too, is arranged in accordance with the soundex system.

4. An alphabetical card index to the City Lists prepared by the WPA. This index is located in the Baltimore City Archives and is open to the public. The original City Lists are also on file here.

Published Lists

The only published work treating passengers landing at the port of Baltimore is *Passenger Arrivals at the Port of Baltimore 1820-1834,* ed. Michael Tepper, transcr. Elizabeth P. Bentley (Baltimore: Genealogical Publishing Company, 1982). The pilot volume in the now defunct *Passenger Arrivals* series—a series which had been designed to document passenger arrivals at the principal ports of entry to the end of the nineteenth century, but New York arrivals only to 1846—it provides access to the records of the 50,000 immigrants who arrived at the port of Baltimore from 1820 to 1834. Owing to gaps in the original passenger lists, the focus of the work is skewed to the early 1830s, particularly 1833-34, when Germans arriving on ships departing from Bremen were in the ascendant. Although arranged in alphabetical order (with a separate index to ships, showing ports of embarkation and dates of arrival), the information given corresponds in virtually all details with the Customs Passenger Lists. The great virtue of the work is that it draws on *all* the available passenger arrival records, linking them together for ease of reference.

New Orleans

Owing to the volume and diversity of its records, it is rather more difficult to get a handle on New Orleans passenger lists than on lists at other ports of entry. Original passenger lists—those submitted to the New Orleans customs collectors—extend roughly from 1820 to January 1903. The National Archives' microfilm edition of these lists (M259) includes copies of the passenger lists, inserted in place of missing or illegible originals, as well as a substantial number of cargo manifests (baggage lists), which furnish names and, occasionally, ages of the passengers. Cargo manifests begin to show up in the microfilm publication in the year 1821 and remain a prominent feature of the microfilmed lists until the final years of the next decade. Quarterly

Abstracts run from 1820 to 1875, and the microfilm publication, M272, includes bound volumes of abstracts for the years 1845-75—presumably maintained in this form by New Orleans customs officials. State Department Transcripts extend from 1820 to 1827, with entries for 1820 listed under the District of Mississippi. Also in the National Archives (but not on microfilm) are five typewritten volumes prepared in the early 1940s by the Work Projects Administration of Louisiana entitled "Passenger Lists Taken from Manifests of the Customs Service, Port of New Orleans, 1813-1867." These volumes, numbered 1-4 and 6, appear to have been copied from cargo manifests and original passenger lists, though the foreword declares ambiguously that the data derives "from manifests which form a portion of the archives of the United States Customs Service stored in the record room of the Customs House in New Orleans." Overall, they run in a slightly irregular pattern and in the early years are decidedly spotty. For example, there are approximately sixty-five cargo manifests and passenger lists for 1813, none for 1814, only about five for 1815, and no other lists until 1821 (although a cargo list of 1817 appears to have been misfiled among the lists for 1821), and there are additional gaps and interruptions in the chronological sequence later on. (Apparently unknown to the National Archives, a carbon copy of the missing fifth volume, as well as a seventh volume, dated 1868-70, is held at the Louisiana Historical Center, 751 Chartres Street, New Orleans, LA 70176.) Adding to the difficulties besetting the New Orleans port arrival records is the fact that numerous passenger lists were written in foreign hands, often on handwritten forms. Considering that a large number of such lists consist of various unfamiliar French, Spanish, and German locutions—to say nothing of passengers' names—they must be accounted among the most difficult for the modern researcher to work with.

As at other ports of entry there are journals of and alphabetical indexes to vessel entrances, which also serve as finding aids to names of vessels and dates of arrival for most of the period 1820-1902 (National Archives Record Group 36).

Indexes

Indexes prepared by the WPA in the 1930s are adequate but not totally comprehensive. Two in the National Archives are on microfilm:

(1) *A Supplemental Index to Passenger Lists of Vessels Arriving at Atlantic and Gulf Coast Ports (Excluding New York), 1820-1874* (M334), which includes New Orleans to about 1850; and (2) *Index to Passenger Lists of Vessels Arriving at New Orleans Before 1900* [i.e. 1853-99] (T527). A third index, also an alphabetical card index and also in the National Archives, covers the period 1900 January 1903, but is not on microfilm.

Published Lists

There is as yet no major published list of passenger arrivals at the port of New Orleans, though there are a number of classified lists that treat passengers by nationality. One of the largest of these to date is Leo Baca's *Czech Immigration Passenger Lists,* 4 vols. (Hallettsville, Tex.: Old Homestead Publishing Co., 1983-91). Compiled from Customs Passenger Lists, this work deals with the records of Czech and Slovak immigrants who arrived not only at New Orleans but at Galveston, New York, and Baltimore. The New Orleans lists cover arrivals prior to 1900, the majority—documenting pre-1880 arrivals—appearing in Volume 1. (Czech passengers arriving at Galveston between 1896 and 1914 are the primary focus of Volumes 2 and 3, while Volume 4 is devoted in entirety to Czechs arriving at New York from 1847 to 1869.) Other classified lists of passenger arrivals at New Orleans (Spanish, French, etc.) are cited in P. W. Filby's *Passenger and Immigration Lists Bibliography 1538-1900* (see p. 40).

OTHER PORTS

Records of the five major ports of entry are so numerous that we can almost be forgiven for overlooking the records of the smaller ports, which even in the aggregate don't come up to very much. By an act of 31 July 1789 customs collection districts were established in more than 100 coastal, river, Great Lakes, and inland ports. (The boundaries changed from time to time until in 1913 a single customs district was established in each state or territory.) Of these officially designated ports of entry, about three-fourths have passenger arrival records of various description, although only Mobile, Alabama, New Bedford,

Massachusetts, and Newport, Rhode Island have original lists of any appreciable quantity. For the rest, copies and abstracts of various dates between 1820 and 1873, State Department Transcripts, and a few scattered originals are all that exist. Copies of the extant passenger lists for most of these ports, together with some original lists for Mobile and Savannah, have been assembled by the National Archives in a sixteen-roll microfilm publication called *Copies of Lists of Passengers Arriving at Miscellaneous Ports on the Atlantic and Gulf Coasts and at Ports on the Great Lakes, 1820-1874* (M575). The lists are arranged by port and the ports arranged in alphabetical order, with roll 3 devoted to Galveston, Texas, and rolls 9-14 to Portland and Falmouth, Maine (from 1847 both were increasingly popular ports of entry for German and Irish immigrants, the former at Galveston, the latter, down from Quebec and the Maritime Provinces, at Portland and Falmouth). All lists are indexed in M334, *A Supplemental Index to Passenger Lists of Vessels Arriving at Atlantic and Gulf Coast Ports (Excluding New York), 1820-1874.*

Although revealing few details on passengers, other administrative records maintained at customs collection districts can sometimes be useful in correlating ship arrival information. These records are a mixed lot, but since they are found at greater and lesser ports alike and contain comprehensive documentation of incoming vessels and cargoes, they demand at least a brief description. The authoritative *Guide to the National Archives of the United States* provides perhaps the best account:

> The records of more than 100 collectors or collection districts that are in the National Archives represent many ports and subports, some discontinued, and consist in general of correspondence, records of the entrance and clearance of vessels, cargo manifests, impost books . . . records relating to warehousing, drawbacks, nonintercourse, embargo, and other bonds, crew lists, accounts of hospital moneys paid and other fiscal records, wreck reports, and a few logbooks of privateer vessels. Records for each district vary in date, type, and completeness. Those for the New England ports and New Jersey contain many records of fishing vessels and fishing bounties; those for Southern ports— especially Mobile, Savannah, and New Orleans—include coastwise slave manifests and records relating to the enforcement of prohibitions on slave trade with foreign

> ports; and those of districts along the Canadian border
> include records of warehousing and transportation. . . .
> Records of the collectors at Charleston, Galveston, Savan-
> nah, Mobile, and New Orleans include some Confederate
> customs records.[5]

Like the passenger lists themselves, the records described above are located in the National Archives in Record Group 36, Records of the U.S. Customs Service.

As we have already seen, original passenger arrival records can occasionally be found outside the National Archives. Optimism shouldn't run away with us on this account, however, since it's not likely many such records exist for the smaller ports of entry. There will be few states that boast, like Massachusetts, of having selected records from more than a half-dozen small ports (it's reported, for instance, that passenger arrival records for 1869-71 for the ports of Gloucester, Lynn, Marblehead, New Bedford, Newburyport, Provincetown, Salem, and Wareham are in the State Archives in Boston), but until a complete inventory is compiled we can't be sure of the extent of these records, nor how they compare with those in the National Archives. In the meantime, an independent investigation of the holdings of local archives may prove worthwhile.

WHERE TO FIND THE RECORDS

As previously stated, the original Customs Passenger Lists for the five major ports of entry are kept at the Temple–Balch Center for Immigration Research in Philadelphia. This is not a public research facility and permission to use the original passenger lists must be obtained on application. The remaining records, both original and microfilm, are available at the National Archives in Washington, where the researcher also has access to card indexes and to microfilm copies of the records now held by the Center. The National Archives is the permanent repository of historically valuable records of the three branches of the federal government, but as it is also a public research institution, there is no question of access to the records, provided the prevailing rule of confidentiality is respected.

Researchers may purchase microfilm by the roll from the National Archives or buy photocopies of single pages of passenger lists, or indeed they may search the records at the Archives for themselves. Passenger arrival records on microfilm are available for research in the Microfilm Research Room in the National Archives building, Pennsylvania Avenue and Eighth Street, N.W.; while those that have not been microfilmed can be used in the Central Research Room at the same location.

Before purchasing microfilm it is advisable to check the National Archives' catalogue of microfilm publications on immigrant and passenger arrivals to see which lists have been filmed. Copies of this catalogue—*Immigrant and Passenger Arrivals: A Select Catalog of National Archives Microfilm Publications*—can be obtained for $2.00 from the National Archives Trust Fund, P.O. Box 100793, Atlanta, Georgia 30384-0793 (make check or money order payable to National Archives Trust Fund and add $3.00 for postage and handling). Institutional orders submitted as official purchase orders can be sent to the Cashier, National Archives Trust Fund, Washington, D.C. 20408. This catalogue is one in a select series that describes National Archives microfilm publications related to specific subjects of high research interest. It contains detailed descriptions of the microfilmed records and roll-by-roll listings for each publication. Positive microfilm copies may be purchased at prices shown in the catalogue. Orders should be submitted on NATF Form 36 (Microfilm Order) or on institutional or commercial purchase order forms, and should include the correct microfilm publication number, roll number, and price. Orders by check or money order should be sent to the Atlanta address given above, while credit card orders should be addressed to the Cashier (NAJC), National Archives Trust Fund, Washington, D.C. 20408. A sample order form, photo-reduced, is shown opposite; full-size copies of the form can be found at the end of the catalogue or obtained on request.

If instead of buying an entire roll of microfilm the researcher would prefer to have copies of single pages of passenger lists, it may be possible for the Archives to supply a photocopy. However, the Archives can only provide this service if precise identifying information is given them. At the risk of repeating ourselves (although it really can't be emphasized too strongly), we again note the Archives' requirements and quote in full from the introduction to the catalogue of microfilm publications cited above.

MICROFILM ORDER
(Prices subject to change.)

Microfilm publication numbers (preceded by an "M" or "T") are assigned to each microfilm publication. Please enter the microfilm publication number and roll number(s) in the proper columns. Because we accept orders for individual rolls, as well as for complete microfilm publications, we must know which rolls you wish to purchase.

Effective August 1, 1990, the price for each roll of microfilm is $23 for U.S. orders. The price is $30 per roll for foreign orders. Shipping is included. These prices are subject to change without notice. For current price information, write to the Publications Services Staff (NEPS), National Archives and Records Administration, Washington, DC 20408, or call 202-501-5240.

Sample of correctly completed form.

MICRO. PUB. NUMBER	ROLL NUMBER(S)	PRICE
T624	1138	$23.
T1270	88 - 89	$46.

Additional order forms are available upon request.

ORDERED BY *(Include organization if shipping to a business address.)*	Name
	Organization *(if applicable)*
	Address *(Number and Street)*
	City, State & ZIP Code
	Daytime Telephone Number *(Include area code)*

PAYMENT TYPE

CREDIT CARD — Check one and enter card number below. ☐ VISA ☐ MasterCard

Exp. Date

Signature

OTHER — ☐ Check ☐ Money Order
Make payable to: National Archives Trust Fund.

Amount Enclosed $

Send your order to:

National Archives Trust Fund Cashier (NAJC) Washington, DC 20408

National Archives Trust Fund P.O. Box 100793 Atlanta, GA 30384-0793

IDENTIFY THE ROLLS YOU WISH TO ORDER

MICRO. PUB. NUMBER	ROLL NUMBER(S)	PRICE		MICRO. PUB. NUMBER	ROLL NUMBER(S)	PRICE
					Subtotal (this column)	
	Subtotal (this column)				Subtotal from first column	
					TOTAL PRICE	

NATIONAL ARCHIVES TRUST FUND BOARD   NATF Form 36 (rev. 4-91)

NATF Form 36, used for ordering microfilm publications from the National Archives.

If the list is indexed, the Reference Services Branch will consult the index to find the correct page of the passenger list to copy. The minimum information required for a search of the index is the full name of the person being researched, the port of arrival, and the approximate date of arrival. Additional information such as age of passenger and names of accompanying passengers can be useful. More specific information, however, is needed to search unindexed lists. In addition to the facts listed above, it is necessary to provide *either* the *exact* date of arrival *or* the name of the ship on which the person arrived.

Requests for these copies must be made on NATF Form 81, "Order for Copies of Passenger Arrival Records." The fee for this service is $10, payable only when the records requested are found. If it is not possible to find records, no payment is required. The order form can be obtained from the Reference Service Branch (NNRS), National Archives, Washington, DC 20408.[6]

For researchers outside the Washington, D.C. area, it may be possible to view microfilm copies of selected Customs Passenger Lists at one of the twelve regional archives of the National Archives which serve citizens across the country. Set up to house federal records outside the Washington area—records of regional offices of federal agencies, for example, and of U.S. District and Circuit Courts—the regional archives also maintain microfilm copies of some of the key records located at the Archives in Washington. While no regional archives branch holds a copy of every microfilm publication, or even of every microfilm publication relating to the region served, most branches have *some* microfilmed Customs Passenger Lists. The following is a list of National Archives regional archives and the regions they serve.

REGIONAL ARCHIVES OF THE NATIONAL ARCHIVES

**National Archives–
New England Region**
380 Trapelo Road
Waltham, MA 02154

Serves Connecticut, Maine,
Massachusetts, New Hampshire,
Rhode Island, and Vermont

National Archives–Northeast Region
201 Varick Street
New York, NY 10014

Serves New Jersey, New York,
Puerto Rico, and the Virgin Islands

**National Archives–
Mid-Atlantic Region**
5000 Wissahickon Avenue
Philadelphia, PA 19144

Serves Delaware, Pennsylvania,
Maryland, Virginia, and
West Virginia

**National Archives–
Great Lakes Region**
7358 South Pulaski Road
Chicago, IL 60629

Serves Illinois, Indiana, Michigan,
Minnesota, Ohio, and Wisconsin

National Archives–Southeast Region
1557 Saint Joseph Avenue
East Point, GA 30344

Serves Alabama, Georgia, Florida,
Kentucky, Mississippi, North
Carolina, South Carolina, and
Tennessee

**National Archives–
Central Plains Region**
2306 East Bannister Road
Kansas City, MO 64131

Serves Iowa, Kansas, Missouri, and
Nebraska

**National Archives–
Southwest Region**
501 West Felix Street
PO Box 6216
Fort Worth, TX 76115

Serves Arkansas, Louisiana, New
Mexico, Oklahoma, and Texas

**National Archives–
Rocky Mountain Region**
Building 48, Denver Federal Center
Denver, CO 80225

Serves Colorado, Montana, North
Dakota, South Dakota, Utah, and
Wyoming

**National Archives–
Pacific Sierra Region**
1000 Commodore Drive
San Bruno, CA 94066

Serves northern California, Hawaii,
Nevada (except Clark County), and
the Pacific Ocean area

**National Archives–
Pacific Southwest Region**
24000 Avila Road
PO Box 6719
Laguna Niguel, CA 92677

Serves Arizona, the southern
California counties of Imperial, Inyo,
Kern, Los Angeles, Orange,
Riverside, San Bernadino, San
Diego, San Luis Obispo, Santa
Barbara and Ventura, and Clark
County, Nevada

**National Archives–
Pacific Northwest Region**
6125 San Point Way, N.E.
Seattle, WA 98115

Serves Idaho, Oregon, and
Washington

National Archives–Alaska Region
Federal Office Building
654 West Third Avenue, Room 012
Anchorage, AK 99501

Serves Alaska

Microfilm copies of Customs Passenger Lists may also be found at various public and university libraries and at historical societies located within proximity of the major ports of entry, but there is only one institution other than the Archives itself that has holdings of virtually all the microfilmed records—the Family History Library of The Church of Jesus Christ of Latter-day Saints in Salt Lake City. Boasting probably the largest collection of records in the world outside government, the Family History Library has records on over one billion people on 1.7 million rolls of microfilm (equal to about 6 million printed volumes) and 325,000 microfiche. The LDS generously makes its records available to Mormons and non-Mormons alike, and its Salt Lake City facility welcomes several thousand visitors daily. A list of library services and a list of the several hundred LDS branch libraries (family history centers) at which microfilm may be ordered and viewed can be obtained by writing to the Family History Library, 35 North West Temple Street, Salt Lake City, Utah 84150. A microfiche copy of the Library's catalogue, the Family History Library Catalog (FHLC), is available at all LDS family history centers.

There are also various commercial concerns that offer microfilm of the passenger lists on a rental basis, among them the American Genealogical Lending Library, through its sales and marketing arm Historic Resources, Inc., P.O. Box 254, Bountiful, Utah 84011-0254. This organization also sells microfilm by the roll, as does Scholarly Resources, Inc., 104 Greenhill Avenue, Wilmington, Del. 19805-1897. Both companies will supply catalogues on request.

NOTES

1. U.S. Congress. Senate. *Reports of the Immigration Commission,* vol. 39 *(Federal Immigration Legislation).* 61st Cong., 3d sess., S. Doc. 758 (Washington, D.C.: Government Printing Office, 1911), 341.

2. *Guide to Genealogical Research in the National Archives,* rev. ed. (Washington, D.C.: National Archives and Records Service, 1985), 41.

3. *Immigrant and Passenger Arrivals: A Select Catalog of National Archives Microfilm Publications,* 2nd ed. (Washington, D.C.: National Archives Trust Fund Board, 1991), 18.

4. For a critical appraisal of *Germans to America* see Michael P. Palmer, "Published Passenger Lists: A Review of *German Immigrants* and *Germans to America,*" *German Genealogical Society of America Bulletin* (May/August 1990): 69-90. An interesting analysis of both *Germans to America* and *The Famine Immigrants* is found in Gordon L. Remington, "Feast or Famine: Problems in the Genealogical Use of *The Famine Immigrants* and *Germans to America,*" *National Genealogical Society Quarterly* (June 1990): 135-46.

5. *Guide to the National Archives of the United States* (Washington, D.C.: National Archives and Records Service, 1974), 169-70.

6. *Immigrant and Passenger Arrivals: A Select Catalog,* 2.

Table 1

CUSTOMS PASSENGER LISTS IN THE NATIONAL ARCHIVES

Adapted from Guide to Genealogical Research in the National Archives
Rearranged and Brought up to Date

PORT OR DISTRICT	ORIGINALS	COPIES OR ABSTRACTS	STATE DEPT. TRANSCRIPTS
Alexandria, Va.		1820-65*	1820-31
Annapolis, Md.		1849*	
Baltimore, Md.[1]	1820-91 (gaps) M255	1820-69 (gaps) M596	1820, 22-27, 29
Bangor, Me.		1848*	
Barnstable, Ma.		1820-26*	1820-26
Bath, Me.	Apr 1806	1825, 27, 32, 67*	
Beaufort, N.C.		1865*	
Belfast, Me.		1820-31, 51*	1820, 22-24, 27, 29, 31
Boston, Ma.[2]	1 Jan 1883-29 Jul 1891 M277; 1891-99, 1912	22 Sep 1820 - 31 Mar 1874 (gaps) M277	1820-27

* Available in National Archives microfilm publication M575; indexed in M334.

[1] M255 indexed in M327, except for City Lists (1833-66) which are indexed separately in M326. M596 is unindexed, but *copies* of passenger lists to about 1870 are indexed in M334.

[2] 1820-74 (M277) indexed in M334; 1848-91 (State Lists) indexed in M265.

Table 1—*Continued*

Port or District	Originals	Copies or Abstracts	State Dept. Transcripts
Bridgeport, Ct.		1870*	
Bridgetown, N.J.		1828*	
Bristol & Warren, R.I.		1820-25, 28, 43-71*	
Cape May, N.J.		1828*	
Charleston, S.C.		1820-28*	1820-29
Darien Ga.		1823, 25*	
Dighton, Ma.		1820-36* (gaps)	1819, 23, 26, 28
East River, Va.		1830*	1830
Edenton, N.C.		1820*	1820
Edgartown, Ma.		1820-70*	1820-28, 31-32
Fairfield, Ct.		1820-21*	1820
Fall River, Ma.		1837-65* (gaps)	
Frenchman's Bay, Me.		1821, 26-27* (gaps)	1822, 25-27
Galveston, Tx.		1846-71*	
Georgetown, D.C.		1820-21*	1820
Gloucester, Ma.	Dec 1905	1820, 32-39, 67-68, 70*	
Hampton, Va.		182-*	
Hartford, Ct.		1832*	
Havre de Grace, Md.		1820*	
Hingham, Ma.		1852*	

Table 1—Continued

PORT OR DISTRICT	ORIGINALS	COPIES OR ABSTRACTS	STATE DEPT. TRANSCRIPTS
Kennebunk, Me.		1820-27, 42*	1820, 22-25, 27
Key West, Fl.		1837-52, 57-68*	
Little Egg Harbor, N.J.		1831*	
Marblehead, Ma.		1820-36, 49*	1821-23, 25-27
Middletown, Ct.	1822-33		
Mobile, Al.[3]	1820-79 (gaps) M575	1832, 49-52 (gaps)	1820-23
Nantucket, Ma.		1820-51, 57-62*	1820, 22-25, 29, 31
Newark, N.J.		1836*	
New Bedford, Ma.[4]	1823-99	1826-52* (gaps)	1822, 25-27, 30-31
New Bern, N.C.		1820-45, 65*	1820-30
Newburyport, Ma.		1821-39* (gaps)	1821-31
New Haven, Ct.		1820-73* (gaps)	1822-31
New London, Ct.		1820-47* (gaps)	1820, 23-27, 29, 31
New Orleans, La.[5]	1820-Jan 1903 M259	1820-75 M272; 1819-90, 74-92, 97-98	1820-27
Newport, R.I.	1820-75 (gaps)	1820-52, 57*	1820-28

[3] Indexed to 1874 in M334.

[4] The Archives has an unmicrofilmed card index for New Bedford, 1875-99.

[5] M259 indexed to about 1850 in M334; 1853-99 indexed in T527.

Table 1—*Continued*

Port or District	Originals	Copies or Abstracts	State Dept. Transcripts
New York, N.Y.[6]	1820-17 Jun 1897 M237; 1840-74, 75-97	1820-74	1820-27
Norfolk & Portsmouth, Va.		1820-57*	1820-32
Oswegatchie, N.Y.		1821-23*	1821-23
Passamaquodcy, Me.		1820-59*	1822-26, 31
Penobscot, Me.		1851*	
Perth Amboy, N.J.	1801-37 (gaps)	1820, 29-32*	1829
Petersburg, Va.		1820-21*	1819-20, 22
Philadelphia, Pa.[7]	1800-82 M425; 1883-99	1820-54; Aug. 1898, 1900-05	1820-22, 24-27, 29
Plymouth, Ma.		1821-36, 43*	1822, 24, 26-27, 29-30
Plymouth, N.C.		1820, 25, 40*	1820, 23
Portland and Falmouth, Me.		1820-24, 26-53, 56-68*	1820-32
Port Royal, S.C.		1865*	
Portsmouth, N.H.		1820-22, 24, 26-33, 35-37, 42-52, 57-61*	1820, 22, 24-31
Port Townsend & Tacoma, Wa.	1894-1909 M1484		

[6] M237 indexed to 1846 in M261.
[7] M425 indexed in M360; 1820-74 indexed in M334.

Table 1—Continued

Port or District	Originals	Copies or Abstracts	State Dept. Transcripts
Providence, R.I.	1820, 22-31	1820-32, 34-35, 37, 39, 41-52, 57-62, 64-67*	1820-28, 30-31
Provincetown, Ma.	1887-89, 93, 95-96		
Richmond, Va.		1820-24, 26-30, 32, 36-37, 44*	1820-24, 28, 30
Rochester, N.Y.		1866*	
Sag Harbor, N.Y.		1829, 32, 34*	1829
St. Augustine, Fl.		1821-22, 24, 27, 70*	1822-24, 27
St. Johns, Fl.		1865*	
Salem & Beverly, Ma.	1798, 1800	1865-66*	1823
Sandusky, Oh.		1820*	1820
San Francisco, Ca.	1903-18 M1412		
Savannah, Ga.	1820-26*	1820-22, 24-26, 31, 47-51, 65-67*	1820-23, 25-26, 31
Saybrook, Ct.		1820*	
Waldoboro, Me.		1820-21, 33*	1820-21
Washington, N.C.		1828-31, 36-37, 48*	1828-29, 31
Wilmington, De.[8]		1820, 30-31, 33, 40-49*	1820
Wiscasset, Me.			1819, 29
Yarmouth, Me.		1820*	

[8] State Department Transcripts entered under the District of Delaware.

IMMIGRATION PASSENGER LISTS

THE BEGINNING OF MASS MIGRATION

When legislation was approved in March 1819 regulating passenger ships arriving at American ports from abroad, it is doubtful whether anyone in Congress could have foreseen the magnitude of immigration to the United States a quarter-century later. In 1820, for instance, the first year in which official passenger lists were kept, fewer than 10,000 passengers arrived at Atlantic and Gulf Coast ports from abroad; but by 1846, the first year of the Great Famine in Ireland, the number of arrivals at the port of New York alone reached nearly 100,000, and at the same port, just five years later, the number swelled to almost 300,000. Events in Europe and opportunities in America were contributing factors, but the catastrophe that struck Ireland—the total failure of the potato crop—was the chief cause of this dramatic increase in immigration.

Although there had been warning signals the year before, the blight that decimated the potato crop during the winter of 1845-46 brought ruin to thousands of smallholders and tenant farmers and reduced virtually all of Ireland to poverty. Dependent on the potato not only as the staple of his diet but as a means of barter and paying rent, the Irish peasant was forever at the mercy of his crop; yet accustomed as he was to the natural cycles of bounty and dearth, nothing could have prepared him for the calamity of the Great Potato Famine. When the blight struck—and it struck again in 1848 with even more devastating force—it brought total destruction to the primitive agrarian economy of the island. There was no means of counteracting it, no known chemical agent that could retard it; nor was there an alternative crop that could be quickly sown and harvested.

Despite attempts at reform, few Irish farmers owned their own land or held title to their cottages and cabins, and when the crop failed they had no means whatever of satisfying their remorseless landlords or the hated money lenders. Rents and obligations fell into arrears, and before long there were wholesale evictions throughout much of the country. Thousands of families were thrown on the meagre resources of local jurisdictions or roamed the countryside in search of food. For many of these wretched cottiers—homeless and without any means of sustenance, in dread of the hunger and disease which ultimately claimed the lives of a million of their countrymen—the choice was clear: quit Ireland or perish. Of necessity, therefore, hundreds of thousands chose to leave, and during the epochal period from 1846 to 1851 more than a million men, women, and children emigrated to the United States and Canada, in the majority of cases through the port of New York.

Like no single event before it or after it, the Famine put its stamp on what we have come to think of as mass migration. It embraced emigration as a means of deliverance, shaped attitudes towards it, ritualized it, even gave it its own myths and language. Talk of sailing packets and steerage decks, remittances and paid-up fares, emigration agents and ship brokers, crimps and touts, runners and man-catchers was common coin, and much of the apparatus of mass migration was brought into place—booking offices, quayside lodging houses, medical stations, customs inspections, emigration commissions—the lot thrown together to service the departure for the New World.

After the Famine the perception of America as a place of refuge grew into an unshakable conviction. America was not only a land of economic opportunity, of political and religious freedom, but an asylum, a sanctuary from the contradictory and capricious actions of man and nature. The exodus from Ireland, foreshadowing the great migrations from southern and eastern Europe in the last quarter of the century, thus became a metaphor for the forces which came to bear on some of those later migrations—want, persecution, desperation. The search for asylum wasn't new, but after the Famine the scale and particularly the character of emigration took on a different meaning.

At virtually the same time as the Famine in Ireland, German agriculture also suffered reverses. The distress this occasioned wasn't as decisive a factor as it was in Ireland, since German farmers weren't tied to a single crop, but in combination with other troubles—religious disputes, for instance, caused in part by the compulsory union of the Reformed and Lutheran churches—it figured significantly in the mounting emigration from Germany. Yet even with the support of the newly-founded emigration societies *(auswanderungsverein)* and the cooperation of provincial governments, this emigration, large as it was, came nowhere near matching the levels of Irish emigration. Evidence of this is furnished in a report by the Commissioners of Emigration of the State of New York which shows that in the five years from 1847 through 1851, 536,000 Irish immigrants entered the port of New York as against 277,000 Germans. Figures gathered by the State Department (for all U.S. ports of entry) show an even more pronounced difference: 763,000 Irish to 344,000 Germans.[1] (The difference is even greater when it is considered that nationalities other than German are represented in this figure. Germany did not then exist as a sovereign nation, and no doubt some of those designated as "German" were from German-speaking areas outside the fatherland.) Although these figures were to swing the other way during the next five years, and practically reverse themselves in the decade from 1860 to 1870, there is no denying the fact that the Irish dominated the early stages of mass migration.

Fully three-quarters of all Irish emigrants of the period embarked from Liverpool, the thriving English port on the Mersey estuary in Lancashire. The voyage to New York from Liverpool—which had previously flourished on the slave trade and the trade in cotton and timber—usually took from four to six weeks—longer perhaps in the winter months—and at £3 to £4 for steerage accommodations, it was no more expensive to sail from Liverpool than from smaller Irish ports, and in most cases it was just as fast or faster. (In November 1846, for example, the *Yorkshire* made the crossing from Liverpool to New York in just sixteen days, supposedly the fastest time ever achieved by a packet.) Passage across the Irish Sea to Liverpool could be booked cheaply, or for nothing at all if the passengers were taken on as ballast, and for many emigrants it was simply more expedient to cross the sea than to travel overland to the nearest port at home where departures were less frequent and accommodations uncertain. At the same time there was a general belief that passengers would be better provided for in the larger vessels departing from Liverpool, and although this was not entirely accurate, particularly since the British passenger act of 1842 had diluted health and safety requirements, it was certainly true that such vessels were superior to the decrepit "coffin ships" putting out from the coastal ports of Ireland. Liverpool was in any case a flourishing seaport, the heart of Britain's trans-Atlantic trading empire, and in both ships and services it offered the emigrant a greater range of choice than any other port. Equally important, the great thousand-ton packets putting out of Waterloo Docks were sufficiently seaworthy to transport their human cargo in fair weather and foul, in-season or out, and so offered a distinct advantage to emigrants forced to take flight at unseasonable times of the year.

The majority of vessels in the Liverpool–New York trade carried between 200 and 300 passengers, and some half-dozen or more were regularly carrying 400 to 500. The better ones—the Black Star Line's *Washington* (1,655 tons), the Red Star's *Phoenix* (1,487 tons), and the Black Ball's *Montezuma, Yorkshire,* and *Isaac Webb*—were full-rigged vessels of deep draft and wide beam, generally well-skippered and built to carry large numbers of passengers at a respectable speed. But despite these attractions, demand for them on the Atlantic run was of relatively short duration. Even though many had been specially built for the emigrant trade—the popular American packets, in particular—they were supplanted within a few short years by the faster and more dependable steamship. Lower fares notwithstanding, by the 1860s these leviathans were all but gone as carriers of emigrants. To the refugees of the Famine, therefore, belongs one more dubious distinction —that of being the last major emigrant group to embark under sail.

The first ship to cross the Atlantic using steam as its main motive power is thought to have been a Canadian ship, the *Royal William,* which in 1833 made the journey from Pictou, in Nova Scotia, to London in twenty-five days. (Sometimes credited with being first, the American ship *Savannah,* fitted with steam and sails, crossed the Atlantic in 1819, but mostly under sail.)[2] In spite of their obvious advantages—their speed, safety, and reliability—the first steamships to ply the Atlantic were employed as mail carriers rather than passenger ships. The Cunard Line, for instance, founded in 1840, was subsidized by the British government to carry mail, and ten years later the Collins Line was awarded a subsidy from Congress for the same purpose. Indeed, steamships played almost no part in the transportation of passengers—other than cabin passengers—until 1850 when the Inman Line began to carry immigrants in its iron-hulled screw ships. Inman's ships made regular fortnightly sailings, more than halving the conventional sailing time, and thus brought about an improvement in conditions which legislation had so far failed to achieve. "As soon as the voyage was more than cut in half," notes Terry Coleman in *Going to America*, "the emigrant's chance of arriving fit was more than doubled. The steamer had steam and fire to cook with, and could offer regular cooked food with no trouble. As soon as Inman refused, no doubt in his own interest, to accept sick passengers, he was imposing a medical test much stricter than the government ever had. Everyone who could afford to go by steamer did, and as the demand increased so the fares got lower." [3]

The Hamburg-American Line, founded in 1846, added steamers to their fleet in 1856; North German Lloyd, formed from a consolidation of steamship companies operating out of Bremen, begun steam service to New York in 1859; and in 1862, Cunard, which had been in business since 1840, also began to carry steerage passengers. The wide-hulled American packets, the "floating palaces" of the advertisements, as well as the conventional merchant vessels long used as emigrant carriers, quickly lost ground to the steamship. And once the great steamship lines were organized and operating on a competitive basis, the sailing ship, as a carrier of emigrants, became little more than a dinosaur, although the employment of sails to supplement steam power continued almost to the end of the century.

To illustrate the shift from sail to steam we can hardly do better than to quote statistics showing the relative number of passengers carried to New York on steamships and sailing vessels during the period of transition. In 1856, for instance, 136,459 passengers were carried on sailing vessels against 5,111 on steamships. Ten years later, in 1865, the number of passengers carried by steamship for the first time exceeded the number carried under sail, 116,579 to 83,452. And by 1873, the last year for which figures are available, the numbers were turned upside down: 259,573 were carried by steam, 8,715 by sail. [4] As the pace of emigration quickened and the demand for regular scheduling increased, the steamship never looked back.

IMMIGRATION LEGISLATION

In the meantime, passenger and immigration laws struggled to keep pace with events. The act of 1819—the act which regulated the carriage of passengers in ships and vessels entering American ports from abroad and mandated the keeping of passenger arrival records—had been on the books for more than a quarter of a century. Never notably successful in reducing overcrowding, its shortcomings in the face of the rapidly increasing emigration from Ireland had become a mockery. A passenger act of February 1847, however, the first since 1819, made a long overdue attempt at reform by introducing several regulations intended to add to the comfort of steerage passengers. As before, two passengers were allowed for every five tons of the ship's register, but each passenger, depending on the deck he occupied, was also allowed a certain amount of deck space, measured by clear, superficial feet. Provisions were also included which prescribed the number, size, and position of the berths. Furthermore, two children under the age of eight were computed as one adult, and a child under the age of one not counted at all (this provision was repealed in March of the same year, partially reinstated in 1848, then fully restored in the passenger act of 1855). On the face of it this was a reasonable and humane law, but it failed to address the seminal problem of ventilation.

The real cause of death and illness on board ship was the unhealthy state of the steerage. Medical experts had warned for some time that the airless steerage compartments were a breeding-ground for cholera and dysentery, and now, with the dramatic increase in emigration from Ireland, ship fever—which had plagued steerage travel since the earliest days of emigration—grew to alarming proportions, becoming progressively worse as the number of immigrants who were infected when they came aboard ship increased. The scourge reached its peak in 1847 with the deaths at the quarantine station at Grosse Isle, thirty miles below Quebec on the St. Lawrence, of nearly 5,000 passengers, mainly from the effects of typhus and dysentery (estimates of the number of deaths that occurred prior to quarantine and in the hospitals subsequent to quarantine run as high as 15,000). Mindful of events at Grosse Isle, and of lesser tragedies occurring daily aboard ship, Congress enacted a law in May 1848 which expressly provided for the ventilation of steerage quarters. There were to be at least two ventilators for ships carrying 100 passengers, one with an exhaust to carry off foul air, the other a receiving cap to carry down fresh air. Furthermore, there was to be a cooking range on every vessel carrying fifty or more passengers, a privy for every 100 passengers, and a prescribed amount and kind of food. In addition, ships' captains were authorized to enforce standards of cleanliness which would tend to the preservation and promotion of health. Finally, the tonnage check was dropped, and in its place a single standard of measurement was adopted which allowed each passenger a minimum of fourteen superficial feet of deck space. As before, though, ship owners and masters were able to subvert the law by deliberate undercounts in the manifests, and abuses continued.

A more ambitious attempt at reform came in 1855. A Senate select committee had been appointed in December 1853 to investigate steerage conditions and "to consider the causes and the extent of the sickness and mortality prevailing on board the emigrant ships on the voyage to this country, and whether any, and what, legislation is needed for the better protection of the health and lives of passengers on board such vessels."[5] After a painstaking investigation the committee concluded that the passenger acts of 1819, 1847, and 1848 had failed to materially improve the conditions under which emigrants were carried at sea. Their recommendations for reform, presented to Congress in the form of a report and a bill, were adopted with few changes in the sweeping passenger act of 3 March 1855. Far-reaching as this law was in its reforms, however—and it was hailed as a product of the hard-won lessons of the past thirty-five years—it failed in the very thing it hoped most to achieve—to check overcrowding. "Theoretically," remarked the *Report of the Immigration Commission,* "the law provided for increased air space, better ventilation and improved accommodations in the way of berths, cooking facilities, the serving of food, free open-deck space, etc. Although the evil of overcrowding, which had been attended with such disastrous results in former years, appears to have been especially aimed at by the makers of the law, the wording of the act was, unfortunately, such that the provisions relating to the number of passengers to be carried were inoperative, and there was practically no legal restraint in this regard, as far as the United States law was concerned, between 1855 and 1882."[6]

Although it was clear that the intent of the law was to correct the mischiefs occasioned by overcrowding, it was found by the courts, when the matter was taken before them, that the new rules protecting steerage passengers, owing to ambiguities in the language, applied to sailing vessels rather than steamships. In practice, then, since sailing vessels were disappearing as a form of emigrant transport, the passenger act of 1855 did little to redress the evils of overcrowding, which by default became a function of the faster, larger, and altogether safer steamships.

The 1855 act was essentially a consolidating act. It repealed the passenger acts of 1819, 1847, and 1848 while re-enacting those provisions of the earlier acts which were to be retained, among them the requirement that ships' captains were to deliver a list or manifest of all passengers to the collector of the customs district in which the ship arrived. So although the act failed to achieve its principal objective, it did have the virtue of reaffirming this key provision of the act of 1819. Significantly, there was little change in either the wording or the substance of the mandate. The captain was called on to designate the name, age, sex, and occupation of each passenger, the country to which each belonged, that of which it was their intention to become an inhabitant, and whether any and what number had died on the voyage. Except that the captain was now asked to specify the part of the vessel occupied by each passenger during the voyage, this remained the only information furnished on passengers until 1882.

In spite of the anti-Catholic, anti-Irish agitation of the 1840s and 1850s, represented politically by the Native American Party, then, briefly, by the spectacularly successful Know-Nothings, and in spite of the very real threat of cheap foreign labor, no restrictions were placed on immigration until 1875. In that year Congress enacted legislation prohibiting two classes of aliens from entering the country —criminals (other than those convicted of political offenses) and prostitutes. Provision was also made for the inspection of vessels and for the deportation of excluded aliens, thus marking the beginning of direct government intervention in immigration matters. Previously, individual states had restricted the importation of lunatics, idiots, criminals, and paupers, and had imposed head taxes and bonds to indemnify local authorities against charges arising from the care and support of indigent passengers. In 1876, however, in a landmark decision, the Supreme Court declared it unconstitutional for states to regulate immigration and to tax incoming passengers, pointing out that states had no power to interfere with or to regulate foreign commerce (in this instance, the transportation of emigrants), which was the exclusive function of Congress. In the same decision, moreover, the Court recommended that Congress exercise complete control over immigration. A few months later, in July of 1876, bills were introduced in the Senate and the House of Representatives calling for the national regulation of immigration. Although both bills failed, similar measures were regularly introduced by New York senators and congressmen, for in practice the Supreme Court's decision weighed heavily against New York where more than three-quarters of all immigrants landed. Finally, after repeated efforts by New York legislators, a federal immigration law was passed on 3 August 1882 which ameliorated the worst effects of the Supreme Court's decision. As adopted, this, the first general immigration law, provided for a head tax of fifty cents (this would be used by local authorities to defray expenses), charged the Secretary of the Treasury with responsibility for executing the provisions of the act, giving him authority to enter into contracts with state officials for the local administration of immigration, and excluded lunatics, idiots, persons likely to become public charges, and foreign convicts (except those convicted of political offenses). The effect of this law was to place the administrative control of immigration in the hands of the federal government—namely, the Treasury Department, which now had authority to prescribe rules regulating immigration. (Full federal control wasn't completely established, however, until 1891, when the office of Superintendent of Immigration was established under the Treasury Department and given charge of all immigration matters except the Chinese Exclusion Acts).

Not forgotten in the debate which preceded the immigration act of 3 August 1882—and before that (6 May 1882) the first of the Chinese Exclusion Acts—were the shortcomings of the 1855 passenger act. As it was interpreted by the courts, this act failed to provide for the safety and comfort of passengers travelling by steamship, now the predominant if not the sole means of ocean travel. Regulations governing sailing vessels were inapplicable and far too many decisions were left to the discretion of ship owners and masters, especially in matters pertaining to the carriage of passengers on decks which had not even been envisioned by the 1855 law. Accordingly, a new passenger act was drafted to rectify the oversights of the 1855 act and to meet the realities of modern-day immigration (approved 2 August 1882—the day before the immigration act).

Because it was sympathetic to the passengers' welfare, and was at pains to be precise where distinctions between steamships and sailing vessels were in question, the new passenger act was a considerable improvement over its predecessors. To the Immigration Commission of 1911, believing that it had got it right at last, it was an exceptional piece of legislation:

> Viewed from the standpoint of its predecessors the passenger act of 1882 was an excellent measure. Its framers had profited by observing the results of the legislative experiments of about sixty-two years. This advantage, together with the marvelous development and progress in the method of handling passenger traffic, enabled the lawmakers to draft an intelligent and comprehensive bill. By its provisions the safety and comfort of emigrants were theoretically, at least, assured. No deck less than 6 feet in height, on any vessel, was allowed to be used for passengers. With the development of shipbuilding, however, other decks were added to ships and this provision soon became obsolete. Sufficient berths for all passengers were to be provided, the dimensions of each berth to be not less than 2 feet in width and 6 feet in length, with suitable partitions dividing them. The sexes were to be properly separated. The steerage was to be amply supplied with fresh air by means of modern and approved ventilators. Three cooked meals, consisting of wholesome food, were to be served regularly each day. Each ship was to have a fully equipped modern hospital for the use of sick passengers. A competent physician was to be in attendance, and suitable medicines were to be carried.[7]

There is little doubt that this act served to improve existing conditions and smooth the way for the great pre-War emigration from Europe. But in addition to the excellent remedial measures incorporated in this act, there was something else: for the first time since 1819 there was a small but significant change in the information required of each passenger in the manifests. Masters of vessels entering American ports from abroad were now called on to furnish a list specifying, for cabin passengers, their names, ages, sex, callings, and *country of which they were citizens;* for steerage passengers, their names, ages, sex, call-ings, *native country, and intended destination or location.* Since 1819, it will be remembered, ships' captains had reported only the country to which each passenger owed allegiance—a very different thing some-times from *native* country, and not a very useful or precise determinant of ethnic origin. Also for the first time, passengers were required to indicate their destination or location.

Minor as these innovations appeared to be, they were a concession to the growing sentiment which favored the restriction of immigration. But this was a passenger act, and it was neither the time nor the place for a radical change in immigration policy. Even so, with a standing committee on immigration in the Senate and a select committee on immigration and naturalization in the House, with both parties now generally favoring some form of restriction, the momentum towards a complete overhaul of immigration policy was building. At the very least, the next piece of legislation would tighten the screws. Not sur-prisingly, the next law, the Immigration act of 1891, was aggressively regulatory. It was also the most restrictive act that had been passed to date. It added polygamists and persons suffering from loathsome or contagious diseases to the excluded classes; prohibited the employment of foreigners whose promise of employment was secured through adver-tisements published in foreign countries (thus strengthening the con-tract labor law of 1885 which had been designed to protect American workers from low wages due to the surplus of labor); prohibited trans-portation companies from soliciting, inviting, or encouraging the immi-gration of aliens except by ordinary means; provided for the inspection of immigrants on the borders of Canada and Mexico; provided for the deportation within a year of arrival of any alien who came into the United States in violation of law; and placed all immigration matters in the hands of the Superintendent of Immigration (after 1895 known as the Commissioner General of Immigration). It also made it the duty of the commanding officer and the agents of the steam or sailing vessel to report the name, nationality, *last residence,* and destination of every "alien immigrant."

So volatile was the issue of immigration, however, that this act was in force for only two years before a new law was introduced to help strengthen its provisions. Over the objections of nativists and racists, over the demands of such restrictionist groups as the American Protective Association, which favored a literacy test to curb the influx of immigrants from southern and eastern Europe, the immigration act of 1893 was designed solely "to bring about a more perfect enforcement of the spirit of the existing law." [8] Nevertheless, while it offered little that was new in respect to restrictions, it did provide for major changes in the passenger manifests—the first truly significant changes since 1819. Indeed, the questions now asked of passengers resulted in more than twice the amount of information previously given in the manifests. In accordance with section 1 of this act (27 Stat. L, 3 March 1893), masters or commanding officers of steamers or sailing vessels were to

> deliver to the proper inspector of immigration at the port lists or manifests made at the time and place of embarkation of such alien immigrants on board such steamer or vessel, which shall, in answer to questions at the top of said lists, state as to each immigrant the full name, age, and sex; whether married or single; the calling or occupation; whether able to read or write; the nationality; the last residence; the seaport for landing in the United States; the final destination, if any, beyond the seaport of landing; whether having a ticket through to such final destination; whether the immigrant has paid his own passage or whether it has been paid by other persons or by any corporation, society, municipality, or government; whether in possession of money, and if so, whether upwards of thirty dollars and how much if thirty dollars or less; whether going to join a relative, and if so, what relative and his name and address; whether ever before in the United States, and if so, when and where; whether ever in prison or almshouse or supported by charity; whether a polygamist; whether under contract, express or implied, to perform labor in the United States; and what is the immigrant's condition of health mentally and physically, and whether deformed or crippled, and if so, from what cause.

Here at last was a really detailed passenger manifest, and one with surprising implications, for it showed just how far the government was prepared to go to come to grips with the immigration problem. In theory, the authorities now had the means of determining whether an immigrant qualified for admission, and once admitted into the country, the means of tracing his movements.

But this was still not sufficient.

In 1903, by which time the Commissioner General of Immigration had been placed under the jurisdiction of the newly-created Department of Commerce and Labor, it was resolved in Congress that "the passenger manifests of vessels carrying immigrants shall be full, detailed, and explicit in all data that may serve in personal identification"— this in order to improve the means whereby undesirable aliens might be traced." Therefore, to the greatly expanded format of the passenger manifests pursuant to the act of 1893, the next major piece of legislation, the immigration act of 3 March 1903, added a category for race. (The principal object of this act was to codify all existing legislation, but at the same time it expanded the classes of aliens to be excluded from immigration, adding, for example, epileptics, anarchists, procurers, professional beggars, persons who had two or more attacks of insanity, and previous deportees.) In June 1906, with the passage of the naturalization act which established the Bureau of Immigration and Naturalization (under the wing of the Department of Commerce and Labor), there was a further refinement: manifests were henceforth to carry a personal description of each immigrant and his birthplace— not merely his country of allegiance or citizenship. And in 1907, in the last major piece of immigration legislation passed before World War I, the format of the passenger list was revised to include the name and address of the nearest relative in the country from which the alien came. Thus, a typical passenger list of, say, 1908 or 1909 (there would be a lag between the adoption of a law and the introduction of new forms) would contain the following information on each passenger: (1) name; (2) age; (3) sex; (4) whether married or single; (5) calling or occupation; (6) whether able to read or write; (7) nationality; (8) race or people; (9) last permanent residence; (10) name and complete address of nearest relative or friend in the country from which the alien came; (11) final destination; (12) whether having ticket through to that destination; (13) by whom passage was paid; (14) whether in possession of $50.00, and if less, how much; (15) whether ever before in the United States, and if so, when and where; (16) whether going to join a relative or friend, and if so, what relative or friend, and his name and complete address; (17) whether ever in prison, almshouse, or insane asylum, or supported by charity, and if so, which; (18) whether a polygamist; (19) whether an anarchist; (20) whether coming by reason of any offer, solicitation, or agreement, express or implied, to perform labor in the United States; (21) condition of health, mental and physical; (22) whether deformed or crippled, and if so the nature, length of time, and cause; (23) height; (24) complexion; (25) color of hair and eyes; (26) marks of identification; and (27) place of birth.

Although the 1907 act expanded the classes of aliens to be excluded from immigration, it was argued that the law was selective rather than restrictive, that the purpose was not to keep people out but to ensure that only the right kind of people got in. Whatever we might think of this argument today, it is worth remembering that the act was not basically exclusionary. A literacy test hadn't been imposed, as was threatened, nor a true means test, and despite the popular feeling that something needed to be done to check the flow of foreigners into the country, immigration from southern and eastern Europe was largely unaffected. Not until 1917 did the exclusionists enjoy an outright triumph with the imposition of a literacy test and the establishment of a "barred zone" which excluded most Asians not already covered by the Chinese Exclusion Acts or the Gentleman's Agreement. And not until the 1921 and 1924 Quota Acts, and their reaffirmation in the McCarran-Walter Act of 1952, was immigration sharply and decisively restricted, albeit with a bias which favored immigration from western and northern Europe.

THE PASSENGER LISTS

Immigration Passenger Lists, the largest body of passenger arrival records in the National Archives after Customs Passenger Lists, are a product of the passenger and immigration acts which had been passed since 1882 when the Treasury Department was given responsibility for the administration of immigration. Classified by the National Archives under Record Group 85, Records of the Immigration and Naturalization Service, Immigration Passenger Lists date generally from the 1890s, though Philadelphia's lists commence as early as 1883. With their contents reflecting the various changes in immigration legislation, these increasingly detailed passenger lists include the names not only of immigrants but of visitors and American citizens returning from abroad (for a number of ports, in fact, there are separate lists for aliens and citizens). In addition to passengers arriving at Atlantic and Gulf Coast ports, they cover passenger arrivals at Pacific Coast ports as well as passengers arriving in the United States from various ports in Canada. Unlike Customs Passenger Lists, the majority are found only on microfilm, as the originals were destroyed by the Immigration and Naturalization Service (INS) after filming.

Broadly speaking, Immigration Passenger Lists are those which were maintained by federal immigration officials in compliance with laws passed in 1882, 1891, 1893, and in years following, though there appears to be no single legislative enactment responsible for all of them and no common starting point. For instance, Philadelphia has Immigration Passenger Lists beginning as early as 1883 which, although classified by the INS and subsequently the National Archives as Immigration Passenger Lists—presumably because they were maintained by immigration officials rather than customs officials—were processed on state forms rather than federal forms and missed out some of the information required by the passenger act of 1882. As a matter of fact, the earliest Immigration Passenger Lists for Philadelphia were compiled in compliance with an act of the Commonwealth of Pennsylvania entitled *An Act for the Relief and Employment of the Poor of the City of Philadelphia*—on forms printed by the steamship lines. Boston and Baltimore Immigration Passenger Lists commence in 1891, initially on forms corresponding to the requirements of the law of 1882; while New Orleans Immigration Passenger Lists commence in 1903, with information taken down in compliance with the act of 1893. Immigration Passenger Lists for the port of New York, next to which all others pale in comparison, begin in June of 1897 on forms also devised in accordance with the requirements of the act of 1893.

This act, incidentally, prescribed the form the manifests were to take and stipulated that they were to contain no more than thirty names. Furthermore, it ordered that manifests were to be verified by the signature or oath of the master or commanding officer of the vessel before the United States consul or consular agent at the port of departure, an innovation that led to the pre-embarkation procedures required by the 1924 Quota Act. Whether by design or expedience, the manifests became instrumental in the immigration process itself. Writing in *Ellis Island: An Illustrated History of the Immigrant Experience*, Mary J. Shapiro notes that "the manifests were a major organizing agent in the processing routine. Immigrants were grouped for inspection according to the numbers on their landing tags (worn prominently on their chests), each number corresponding to a manifest page that listed thirty names. In this way, inspectors could examine thirty immigrants, one at a time, without searching and turning pages." Developing the argument further, and incidentally giving the lie to one of the oldest myths in immigration folklore, Shapiro observes that "scores of immigrants contend that in the inspection process their names were changed or simplified. The legendary name changes, however, have never been documented on paper. Ellis Island inspectors actually had no occasion to write out the immigrants' names. Their job was simply to verify information already written in the ships' manifests."[10] To bear this out, see the photographs herein of the passenger lists of the ships *Palatia* (1897) and *Manilla* (1903) where check marks against the names and columns of data indicate that the passenger lists were almost certainly used for verification purposes.

The INS, in whose official custody the passenger lists have been kept since the early part of the century, began its ambitious program of microfilming the Immigration Passenger Lists shortly after it was brought under the wing of the Justice Department. (Established in 1906 as the Bureau of Immigration and Naturalization, under the Department of Commerce and Labor, and reorganized in 1933 as the Immigration and Naturalization Service, the INS became an agency of the Justice Department in 1940.) In accordance with its official mandate, the records of ten ports were microfilmed—Key West, Savannah, New Orleans, Portland (Me.), Baltimore, Boston, New Bedford (Mass.), New York, Philadelphia, and Providence (R.I.)—these forming the bulk of the Immigration Passenger Lists then in the possession of the INS. The microfilming was carried out over a period of years and was thought to have been largely complete, or at least well in hand, until quite recently when an enormous cache of Immigration Passenger Lists was discovered at the Washington National Records Center in Suitland, Maryland. Among the passenger arrival records discovered there were those for the Pacific Coast ports of San Diego, San Pedro, San Francisco, Portland, Seattle (Port Townsend), Tacoma, and Honolulu, and for the port cities of Galveston, Miami, Newport News, Port Huron, Oswego, and El Paso. These records were previously unknown or, as in the case of San Francisco, were thought to have been destroyed. Many have since been microfilmed by the INS (notably the records for San Francisco, Seattle, and Galveston) and master copies have been turned over to the National Archives. These have been formally accessioned and are now available to the public. Others—mostly crew and passenger lists for smaller ports of entry— continue to be filmed and in due course will be given to the Archives, with proper allowance for the new thirty-year rule of confidentiality.

Like Customs Passenger Lists, Immigration Passenger Lists are arranged first by port of entry, then by date of arrival, and then by ship. To locate information about a particular individual in these voluminous records—as with Customs Passenger Lists—it is necessary to know beforehand the port of entry and the approximate date of arrival—if the records are indexed—and if unindexed the port of entry and either the exact date of arrival or the name of the ship. (For a complete discussion of indexed and unindexed passenger lists and the various methods of retrieving information on individual passengers, see chapter 3, especially pages 68 and 92. Note also that the section headed "Where to Find the Records" applies to Immigration Passenger Lists as well as Customs Passenger Lists. Although quite indispensable to anyone undertaking research in Immigration Passenger Lists, it has been thought best to refer the reader to this section rather than to repeat the information here.)

Much like their predecessors, Immigration Passenger Lists are served by a combination of microfilmed indexes. Some of these take the form of alphabetical card indexes, some soundex indexes, and still others "book indexes," i.e. rough alphabetical lists of passengers made out by the shipping lines and subsequently turned over to the INS (these are usually arranged chronologically by date of arrival and include the passenger's name, age, and destination). To the great relief of the researcher, New York passenger arrival records, unindexed for the fifty years up to 1897, are comprehensively indexed from 1897 to 1948. Because New York completely overshadows the other ports of entry, it is perhaps less useful to talk about the five major ports of entry with regard to Immigration Passenger Lists and their indexes than with the older Customs Passenger Lists, but a brief glance at the microfilmed records of the major ports might not be out of place here, especially as it serves to focus attention on those records which are of primary interest to the student of immigration.

Boston

Immigration Passenger Lists for the port of Boston run from 1 August 1891 to December 1943 (National Archives microfilm publication T843). They were apparently filmed by the INS directly from the bound volumes in which they were originally kept. Book indexes extending from 1 April 1899 to 14 September 1940 cover much of this period. Entries in the book indexes (T790) are arranged chronologically by date of the vessel's arrival, then by class of passenger, and thereunder in rough alphabetical order by the first letter of the passenger's surname. Besides the book indexes, there is an alphabetical card index for the period from 1 January 1902 to 30 June 1906 (T521), and another, in rough alphabetical order, from 1 July 1906 to 31 December 1920 (T617). There are no book indexes for 1901, and there appears to be no index at all for the period from 1891 to 1899.

New York

Immigration Passenger Lists for the port of New York from 1897 to 1957 are found on a staggering 8,892 rolls of microfilm, with some of the later rolls containing *flight* manifests. All are available from the National Archives as microfilm publication T715, which effectively encompasses the later history of mass migration. Three microfilmed indexes cover nearly the entire period: T519 runs from 16 June 1897 to 30 June 1902; T621 from 1 July 1902 to 31 December 1943; and M1417 from 1944 to 1948 (the last two are soundex indexes). Book indexes to New York passenger lists, ranging in date from 1906 to 1942, are also available as a microfilm publication (T612). They are arranged by year, by steamship line, then by the date of the vessel's arrival, and thereunder in rough alphabetical order by the initial letter of the passenger's surname. For an itemized description of the contents of the microfilmed indexes—for New York as well as for other ports of entry—the reader is advised to consult the most recent edition of the National Archives' *Immigrant and Passenger Arrivals: A Select Catalog of National Archives Microfilm Publications.*

It looks increasingly likely that the Ellis Island Restoration Commission will succeed in its goal of developing a computerized index to New

York passenger arrival records from 1892 to 1954, i.e. from the year Ellis Island opened for business as an immigrant depot to the year of its closing, during which period an estimated 17 million immigrants were processed at the facility. Plans announced in 1988 called for a 1992 completion date, when it was anticipated that an electronic index would be available to the public in the Great Hall of the newly restored Main Building at Ellis Island. The Commission's announcement caused something of a stir at the time and attracted a good deal of media attention, but despite widespread interest in the project it proved too ambitious and the target date was not met. Lacking the resources and the tools to manage the project on its own, the Commission, a voluntary, non-profit organization, has reputedly joined forces with the LDS Church and the Temple University–Balch Institute Center for Immigration Research (among other groups), and the likelihood is that they will now succeed in their overall design. While not necessarily the only option available to them, collaborating with such organizations as the LDS, with their renowned technical skills and their unique mission in making records accessible, is almost the only practical way of carrying off such an ambitious project. Watch for developments in the press.

Philadelphia

Filmed from the original volumes, with dates occasionally overlapping, the Philadelphia Immigration Passenger Lists for the period from January 1883 to December 1945 are available as microfilm publication T840. A soundex index (T526) covers this entire period (actually up to 28 June 1948), while book indexes (T791) run from 14 May 1906 to 17 June 1926. The book indexes are arranged by vessel line, thereunder by the date of the vessel's arrival, then, in part, by class of passenger, and finally in rough alphabetical order by the initial letter of the passenger's surname. Also available is the *Index to Passenger Lists of Vessels Arriving at Philadelphia, 1800-1906* (M360), which contains some names from passenger lists for the period from 1883 to 1906.

Baltimore

The microfilm publication of the Baltimore Immigration Passenger Lists (T844) originally ran from 12 December 1891 to 30 November 1909; however, a recently released continuation has extended the coverage to 30 June 1948. (Another micropublication (M1477) covers the brief period from December 1954 to May 1957.) Like the Boston and Philadelphia lists, most of the Baltimore Immigration Passenger Lists were filmed from the bound volumes in which they were stored. Again like Boston and Philadelphia there are overlapping dates, and some of the lists were filmed in reverse order by the INS. A single index serves this period—or most of it—a soundex index for the period from 1897 to July 1952 (T520), but it should be noted that the *Index to Passenger Lists of Vessels Arriving at Baltimore, 1820-1897* (M327) serves as a partial index for the years from 1891 to 1897.

New Orleans

Immigration Passenger Lists for the port of New Orleans run from January 1903 to December 1945 (T905), with baggage lists appearing intermittently in the earlier years. A microfilm card index takes the coverage back to 1900—into Customs Passenger Lists—and forward to 1952.

In addition to the information noted above on the five major ports of entry—one or two ports designated "major" only by custom—details concerning the coverage of microfilmed lists and indexes for the ports of Key West, Savannah, Providence, New Bedford, and Portland, as well as other ports as yet unmicrofilmed, can be found in Table 2, as can details of the recently accessioned passenger lists and indexes for Detroit, Galveston, San Francisco, and Seattle. Not included in this table, however, are the twenty-six rolls of the *Index to Passenger Lists of Vessels Arriving at Miscellaneous Ports in Alabama, Florida, Georgia, and South Carolina, 1890-1924* (T517), since this is arranged alphabetically by name of passenger rather than by port. Also omitted from Table 2 is an itemization of the recently accessioned microfilmed records of Canadian border entries, one of the most important additions to the passenger list canon in recent years. Little known previously, this unusual body of records so completely breaks the mold that it warrants separate discussion here.

CANADIAN BORDER ENTRIES[11]

From 1895, after it had been noted that approximately forty percent of all passengers arriving in Canada were actually bound for the United States, a system of joint inspection of immigrants coming overland from Canada was established. There were no restrictions on immigration to the United States from Canada, yet by the terms of the immigration act of 1891, which significantly expanded the list of excluded classes, many immigrants who crossed the border from Canada would have been denied entry at United States ports. (The low fares offered by Canadian steamship companies and railway lines encouraged many people bound for the United States to travel through Canada. One steamship company, the Hansa Line, plying between Liverpool and Quebec and Montreal, took on passengers in Antwerp and Hamburg and, in cooperation with the Canadian Pacific Railway, offered passage to the United States through Canada to many immigrants who would have been denied direct passage under the 1891 restrictions.) With the understanding that American officials could inspect would-be immigrants on arrival in a Canadian port, United States commissioners of immigration were stationed in Quebec, Halifax, and Montreal in the east, and in Victoria and Vancouver in the west.

District 1 of the Immigration Service, headquartered in Montreal, was established in 1909. At its formation it encompassed the entire Canadian border, but by 1924 it was reduced to Maine, Vermont, New Hampshire, New York, and Sault Ste. Marie, Michigan, as other districts had since been established at Detroit, Winnipeg, Spokane, and Seattle, this last with sub-ports in Vancouver and Victoria. Immigrants who entered the United States through District 1, Montreal and Quebec, were reported statistically in District 1 regardless of where they crossed the border. The headquarters were subsequently moved to St. Albans, Vermont where the records—documenting passengers arriving on vessels at Canadian ports and on trains crossing the frontier into the United States—were microfilmed by the INS in the early 1950s. Microfilm copies of the St. Albans records, 1895-1954, have now been accessioned by the National Archives and are available for public use. These are the first records to fully document the passage of immigrants across the Canadian border into the United States. For the period of peak immigration, 1895 to 1915, the St. Albans records include entries from sub-ports as far west as the state of Washington. The following is a list of the records which are now available on microfilm:

> Index (Soundex) to Canadian Border Entries Through the St. Albans, Vermont, District, 1895-1924 (M1461)
>
> Alphabetical Index to Canadian Border Entries Through Small Ports in Vermont, 1895-1924 (M1462)
>
> Index (Soundex) to Entries into the St. Albans, Vermont, District Through Canadian Pacific and Atlantic Ports, 1924-1952 (M1463)
>
> Manifests of Passengers Arriving in the St. Albans, Vermont, District Through Canadian Pacific and Atlantic Ports, 1895-1954 (M1464)
>
> Manifests of Passengers Arriving in the St. Albans, Vermont, District Through Canadian Pacific Ports, 1929-1949 (M1465)

Table 2, beginning on page 125, with the exceptions noted above, is designed to show the reader the full range of Immigration Passenger Lists in the National Archives. It will be seen almost at once that many of the lists for the smaller ports of entry have not been microfilmed, but as mentioned previously, lists for miscellaneous ports in Alabama, Florida, Georgia, and South Carolina, 1890-1924, have been indexed in microfilm publication T517. Lists and indexes that have been microfilmed are identified by their appropriate microfilm publication numbers, usually, but not always, beginning with the letter *T*. (The letter *M*, which identifies the microfilmed Customs Passenger Lists, is used by the National Archives to signify records of high research value in various disciplines; while *T* is generally used to indicate either an incomplete record series or microfilmed records which have been produced by another federal agency—in this case the INS.) The letters *A* and *C* stand for alien list and citizen list respectively, while *B* is used as the abbreviation for book indexes. Although this table is current at the time of writing, the reader should be aware that new materials are constantly being accessioned by the National Archives from the INS. Waiting to be accessioned, for example, are records of Mexican border crossings, additional records of border crossings from Canada, and an index of New York port arrivals for 1949-54. As these records are processed, inspected for preservation purposes, and duplicated, they will be made available to the public.

NOTES

1. Figures for the port of New York, from Table A of the *Annual Reports of the Commissioners of Emigration of the State of New York, 1847-60,* are taken from Terry Coleman, *Going to America* (published in England as *Passage to America,* 1972; reprint, Baltimore: Genealogical Publishing Company, 1987), 298. State Department figures for individual years are published in U.S. Congress. Senate. *Reports of the Immigration Commission,* vol. 3 *(Statistical Review of Immigration, 1820-1910).* 61st Cong., 3d sess., S. Doc. 756 (Washington, D.C.: Government Printing Office, 1911), 23-24.

2. For a discussion concerning the first ships to cross the Atlantic under steam, see Edwin C. Guillet, *The Great Migration: The Atlantic Crossing by Sailing-Ship Since 1770,* 2nd ed. (Toronto: Univ. of Toronto Press, 1963), 236.

3. *Coleman,* 242. I am indebted to Mr. Coleman for much of the preceding information concerning emigration from Liverpool.

4. U.S. Congress. Senate. *Reports of the Immigration Commission,* vol. 39 *(Federal Immigration Legislation).* 61st Cong., 3d sess., S. Doc. 758 (Washington, D.C.: Government Printing Office, 1911), 363 (hereafter cited as *Report*).

5. *Report,* 355.

6. *Report,* 359.

7. *Report,* 368.

8. *Report,* 42-43.

9. *Report,* 54.

10. Mary J. Shapiro, Ivan Chermayeff, and Fred Wasserman, *Ellis Island: An Illustrated History of the Immigrant Experience* (New York: Macmillan Publishing Company, 1991), 117.

11. Adapted from a handout provided by the National Archives.

Table 2

IMMIGRATION PASSENGER LISTS IN THE NATIONAL ARCHIVES

Adapted from *Guide to Genealogical Research in the National Archives*

Rearranged and Brought up to Date

PORT OR DISTRICT	LISTS	INDEXES
Apalachicola, Fl.	4 Sep 1918-A	
Baltimore, Md.	12 Dec 1891-30 Jun 1948 (T844); 1 Dec 1954-7 May 1957 (M1417)	1897-Jul 1952 (T520)
Boca Grande, Fl.	28 Oct 1912-16 Aug 1935-A	
Boston, Ma.	1 Aug 1891-Dec 1943 (T843)	1 Jan 1902-30 Jun 1906 (T521); 1 Jul 1906-31 Dec 1920 (T617); 1 Apr 1899-14 Sep 1940-B (T790)
Brunswick, Ga.	22 Nov 1904-27 Nov 1939-A; 15 Sep 1923-27 Nov 1939-C	
Carrabelle, Fl.	7 Nov 1915-A	
Detroit, Mi.	1906-1954 (M1473); 1946-1957 (M1479)	
Fernandina, Fl.	29 Aug 1904-7 Aug 1932-A	
Galveston, Tx.[1]	1896-1948 (M1359)	1896-1906 (M1357); 1906-51 (M1358)
Gloucester, Ma.	Oct 1906-Jun 1923; 1 Feb 1930-Dec 1943	

[1] Includes sub-ports of Houston, Brownsville, Port Arthur, Sabine, and Texas City.

Table 2—*Continued*

PORT OR DISTRICT	LISTS	INDEXES
Gulfport, Ms.	Sep 1929-Dec 1943	27 Aug 1904-28 Aug 1954 (T523)
Hartford, Ct.		
Jacksonville, Fl.	18 Jan 1904-17 Dec 1945; 19 May 1922-22 Dec 1945-C	
Key West, Fl.	2 Nov 1898-14 Dec 1945 (T940) ; 1 Feb 1907-2 Oct 1945-C	
Knights Key, Fl.	7 Feb 1908-20 Jan 1912; 6 Feb 1908-23 Jan 1911-C	
Mayport, Fl.	16 Nov 1907-13 Apr 1916-A	
Miami, Fl.	5 Oct 1899-29 Dec 1945; 16 Jan 1904-29 Dec 1945-C	
Millville, Fl.	4 Jul 1916-A	
Mobile, Al.	3 Apr 1904-24 Dec 1945; 4 Aug 1916-24 Dec 1945-C	
New Bedford, Ma.	1 Jul 1902-Jul 1942 (T944)	1 Jul 1902-18 Nov 1954 (T522)
New Orleans, La.	8 Jan 1903-31 Dec 1945 (T905)	1900-1952 (T618)
New York, N.Y.	16 Jun 1897-1957 (T715)	16 Jun 1897-30 Jun 1902 (T519); 1 Jul 1902-31 Dec 1943 (T621); 1944-1948 (M1417); 1906-42-**B** (T612)
Panama City, Fl.	10 Nov 1927-12 Dec 1939-A; 10 Sep 1933-12 Dec 1939-C	
Pascagoula, Ms.		15 Jul 1903-21 May 1935 (T523)

Table 2—Continued

PORT OR DISTRICT	LISTS	INDEXES
Pensacola, Fl.	12 May 1900-16 Jul 1945; 21 Jun 1924-15 Dec 1945-C	
Philadelphia, Pa.	Jan 1883-Dec 1945 (T840)	1 Jan 1883-23 Jun 1948 (T526); 14 May 1906-17 Jun 1926-B (T791)
Port Everglades, Fl.	15 Feb 1932-10 Dec 1945; 29 Jan 1940-5 Dec 1945-C	
Port Inglis, Fl.	29 Mar 1912-2 Jan 1913-A	
Port St. Joe, Fl.	12 Jan 1923-13 Oct 1939-A	
Portland and Falmouth, Me.	29 Nov 1893-Mar 1943 (T1151)	29 Jan 1893-22 Nov 1954 (T524); 1907-30-B (T793)
Providence, R.I.	17 Jun 1911-Jan 1943 (T1188)	18 Jun 1911-5 Oct 1954 (T518); 13 Dec 1911-26 Jun 1934-B (T792)
St. Albans, Vt.	(See discussion in the section on "Canadian Border Entries")	
St. Andrews, Fl.	2 Jan 1916-13 May 1926-A	
St. Petersburg, Fl.	15 Dec 1926-1 Mar 1941	
San Francisco, Ca.[2]	1893-1953 (M1410); 1954-1957 (M1411)	1893-1934 (M1389)

[2] Supplemental lists for San Francisco include *Passenger Lists of Vessels Arriving in San Francisco from Honolulu, 1902-07* (M1440), indexed in M1389; *Passenger Lists of Vessels Arriving at San Francisco from Insular Possessions, 1907-11* (M1438), indexed in M1389; *Customs Passenger Lists of Vessels Arriving at San Francisco, January 2, 1903-April 1, 1918*— classified as Customs records and therefore also included in Table 1—(M1412); *Registers of Chinese Laborers Arriving at San Francisco, 1882-88* (M1413); *Lists of Chinese Passengers Arriving at San Francisco, 1888-1914* (M1414); *Lists of Chinese*

Table 2—Continued

Port or District	Lists	Indexes
Savannah, Ga.	5 Jun 1906-6 Dec 1945 (T943); Feb 1943-6 Dec 1945-C	
Seattle, Wa.[3]	1890-1957 (M1383); 1949-54 (M1398)	
Tampa, Fl.	2 Nov 1898-30 Dec 1945; 13 Feb 1907-31 Dec 1945-C	
West Palm Beach, Fl.	8 Sep 1920-21 Nov 1945; 27 Mar 1923-15 Dec 1945-C	

Applying for Admission to the United States Through the Port of San Francisco, 1903-1947 (M1476); *Alien Crew Manifests of Vessels Arriving at San Francisco, Sept. 1, 1896-Sept. 24, 1921* (M1436); *Crew Lists of Vessels Arriving at San Francisco, December 28, 1905-October 30, 1954* (M1416).

[3] Includes Port Townsend and Tacoma as well as the sub-ports of Anacortes, Blaine, Port Angeles, Aberdeen, Gray's Harbor, Everett, Friday Harbor, Bellingham, South Bend, Raymond, Port Wells, Port Bernard, and Princeton. From July 1917 monthly lists of individuals applying for admission to the United States from Canada are interfiled with the vessel arrival records. These lists document Canadian entries through Marcus, Oroville, and Sumas, Washington, and Gateway and Sweet Grass, Montana, all of which were included in the Seattle INS district. Supplemental passenger lists for Seattle include *Lists of Chinese Passengers Arriving at Seattle (Port Townsend), 1882-1916* (M1364); *Certificates of Head Tax Paid by Aliens Arriving at Seattle from Foreign Contiguous Territory, 1917-24* (M1365); *Crew Lists of Vessels Arriving at Seattle, Washington, 1903-17* (M1399); *Customs Passenger Lists of Vessels Arriving at Port Townsend and Tacoma, Washington, 1894-1909*—classified as Customs records and therefore also included in Table 1—(M1484); and *Passenger Lists of Vessels Arriving at Seattle, Washington, from Insular Possessions, 1908-1917* (M1485). The Seattle lists are not as yet indexed.

APPENDIX A

The Hamburg Emigration Lists

Records of departure from European ports in the nineteenth and early twentieth centuries have no common foundation in law, so it is not surprising that they are uneven in coverage or that for certain ports there is no documentation at all. Liverpool, for instance, which serviced more American-bound emigrants than any other port in the nineteenth century, has no departure records of any description until 1890 (after this date they can be found in the records of the Board of Trade in the Public Record Office at Kew). At a number of ports, however, as at Malmö and Göteborg in Sweden, at Le Havre in France, Antwerp in Belgium, Rotterdam in Holland, and at Bremen and Hamburg in Germany, efforts were made to keep tabs on emigrants—if only for statistical purposes or as a means of curbing criminal activity at the port—and records of one kind or another can usually be found. There are police registers of emigrants embarking from Malmö and Göteborg from 1869 to 1951, for instance, and lists of passengers sailing from Le Havre, 1750-1898, on ships under French flag, but nowhere was this kind of record-keeping pursued more energetically than at the ports of Bremen and Hamburg, the chief departure points for millions of emigrants from central and eastern Europe. It has been estimated that 70 percent of all emigrants leaving these ports went to America and that as many as half of all Russian Jews emigrating to America between 1880 and 1914 left via Hamburg alone.

The unhappy fate of the Bremen records is well known. Owing to a lack of space, all the records from their inception in 1832 until 1872 were destroyed in 1874, and from that date on the authorities retained only the lists for the current year and the two most recent years, a practice that stopped in 1909 when the original lists were again maintained on a permanent basis. In 1931 the surviving lists (from 1907 onwards) were deposited with the Statistical Land Office in Bremen where they were destroyed in an Allied bombing raid on 6 October 1944. Transcripts of lists for 1907-08 and 1913-14 were recently discovered at the German State Archives in Koblenz, but no transcripts of nineteenth-century lists have ever come to light. The loss of these records is a serious blow to anyone seeking to develop information on European origins. Bremen is believed to have handled more than twice as many emigrants as Hamburg, and its priceless records can now only be reconstructed from the passenger arrival records in the National Archives (see, for example, the partial reconstructions published by Zimmerman and Wolfert noted on p. 80). Researchers are thus denied a rich booty and must make do with passenger arrival records which—until 1882, at any rate—are usually inferior to the original departure records.

The Hamburg records are a different story, however. Unlike the Bremen records, they are completely intact, and with details on some five to six million persons it is probable that they are the largest body of emigration records in existence. According to Hamburg's Historic Emigration Office,

> Hamburg had long been a commercial center, but also one with a conscience. In 1850 the "Hamburg Association for the Protection of Emigrants" was founded to protect the city's migrant guests. Five years later the city enacted far-reaching legislation: Emigrants were counseled, fed and given medical care, housing for up to 5,000 was constructed. But above all, every ship's agent was required to give the authorities a complete list of all passengers, with names, sex, age, occupation and home city. This list was the origin of the Emigrant Lists, a treasure of America's heritage which has survived intact until today. [Quoted from a leaflet furnished by the Historic Emigration Office.]

The lists date from 1850 to 1934 (with the exception of January-June 1853 and August 1914-1919) and usually list the name of the emigrant, his age, birthplace or former place of residence, occupation, sex, date of departure, ship, and sometimes his marital status, children, and destination. Passengers sailing from Hamburg could choose either a direct or indirect passage to America (the indirect route, via Hull,

Liverpool, Southampton, Rotterdam, etc., was cheaper), and in consequence the records are divided into "direct" and "indirect" categories. The direct passenger lists cover the years 1850 to 1934, with gaps as noted, and the indirect lists 1854 to 1910, after which year they are combined with the direct lists. Indexes of various descriptions exist for both groups of records, but in no case are these indexes comprehensive. An index to the direct lists prepared in Germany by volunteers of the Church of Jesus Christ of Latter-day Saints, for example, runs only from 1856 to 1871. (Entries in the direct lists for 1850-54 are arranged alphabetically by the first letter of the surname of the head of the family, hence there are no indexes for these years.) Again, an index to the direct lists prepared by German emigration officials for 1855-1914 is arranged by year but thereunder only by the first letter of the surname. (The index for 1920-28, however, is in strict alphabetical order.) Furthermore, children and wives (unless the latter were heads of families) are not indexed at all until 1884/1885. An index to the indirect lists, covering the years 1855 to 1910, subject to the same limitations as the direct index, is also available.

The original emigration lists and indexes are housed in the State Archives in Hamburg. Microfilm copies of the lists are located in the Historic Emigration Office in Hamburg and also in the Family History Library of the Church of Jesus Christ of Latter-days Saints in Salt Lake City. Copies of the indexes are also held by the LDS, but probably the best way of getting information from the emigration lists—given the limitations of the indexes—is to contact the Historic Emigration Office in Hamburg, since this organization was set up for the express purpose of dealing with such inquiries. There is of course a charge for the service (at the time of writing $30.00 for each year and name searched). Write to them at the following address:

Historic Emigration Office
c/o Tourist Information am Hafen
Bei den St.-Pauli-Landungsbrücken 3
P.O. Box 102249
D-2000 Hamburg 36
Germany

Also available at the State Archives in Hamburg, supplementing the emigration lists (and available also on microfilm at the Family History Library in Salt Lake City), are (1) emigrant ships' departure registers, 1850-1914; (2) Hamburg police registers of emigrants departing on ships with fewer than twenty-five passengers, 1871-87; and (3) various records of comparatively minor importance, including registers of the Hamburg residents registration office, passport registers, and registers of non-citizen workers. These last have distinctly less value for immigration research than the Hamburg emigration lists, but they are cited here to give some indication of the breadth of records available at the Hamburg State Archives. For more information regarding the holdings of the State Archives see Jürgan Sielemann, "Lesser Known Records of Emigrants in the Hamburg State Archives," *Avotaynu* (Fall 1991); for an informative discussion concerning the research value and methods of using the Hamburg emigration lists see the article by Daniel M. Schlyter, "Hamburg Passenger Lists," in *The Encyclopedia of Jewish Genealogy,* Vol. I, ed. Arthur Kurzweil and Miriam Weiner (Northvale, N.J.: Jason Aronson Inc., 1991).

APPENDIX B

Checklist of Passenger List Publications*

Given below is a list of the principal passenger list publications mentioned in this book in the text and notes. It is not a bibliography (for which see Filby), but merely a checklist of the key books and articles underpinning the narrative. Since it includes most of the important publications that have so far been developed from passenger and immigration records, it is hoped that it can be used as a guide to basic books. Several books not cited in the text but important enough to be featured in a list of basic books are also included. Many of the passenger lists published in books and articles mentioned in this work can be located in the various compilations by Carl Boyer and Michael Tepper which are noted below.

Baca, Leo. *Czech Immigration Passenger Lists*. 4 vols. Hallettsville, Tex.: Old Homestead Publishing Co., 1983-91.

Baird, Charles W. *History of the Huguenot Emigration to America*. 2 vols. 1885. Reprint (2 vols. in 1). GPC, 1973.

Banks, Charles Edward. *The English Ancestry and Homes of the Pilgrim Fathers Who Came to Plymouth on the "Mayflower" in 1620, the "Fortune" in 1621, and the "Anne" and the "Little James" in 1623*. 1929. Reprint. GPC, 1962.

―――. *The Planters of the Commonwealth: A Study of the Emigrants and Emigration in Colonial Times: To Which are Added Lists of Passengers to Boston and to the Bay Colony; the Ships Which Brought Them; Their English Homes, and the Places of Their Settlement in Massachusetts*. 1930. Reprint. GPC, 1961.

―――――

*For simplicity, all books in this list published by the Genealogical Publishing Company of Baltimore are cited *GPC*. In the case of a reprint edition, the earliest reprint date is given.

————. *The Winthrop Fleet of 1630: An Account of the Vessels, the Voyage, the Passengers.* . . . 1930. Reprint. GPC, 1961. This and the previous entry are not cited in the text and notes, but as they are natural extensions of the first Banks entry and are basic works on early New England immigrants, they are included in the checklist.

————. "Scotch Prisoners Deported to New England by Cromwell, 1651-52." *Massachusetts Historical Society Proceedings* 61 (1928): 4-29.

Boyer, Carl, 3rd. *Ship Passenger Lists: National and New England (1600-1825).* Newhall, Calif.: the compiler, 1977.

————. *Ship Passenger Lists: New York and New Jersey (1600-1825).* Newhall, Calif.: the compiler, 1978.

————. *Ship Passenger Lists: The South (1538-1825).* Newhall, Calif.: the compiler, 1979.

————. *Ship Passenger Lists: Pennsylvania and Delaware (1641-1825).* Newhall, Calif.: the compiler, 1980.

Brandow, James R. *Omitted Chapters from Hotten's Original Lists of Persons of Quality.* GPC, 1982.

Brock, Robert A. *Documents, Chiefly Unpublished, Relating to the Huguenot Emigration to Virginia and to the Settlement at Manakin-Town.* . . . 1886. Reprint. GPC, 1962.

Cameron, Viola R. *Emigrants from Scotland to America, 1774-1775.* 1930. Reprint. GPC, 1959.

Childs, St. Julien R.: "The Petit-Guérard Colony." *South Carolina Historical and Genealogical Magazine* 43 (1942): 1-17, 88-97.

Coldham, Peter Wilson. *English Estates of American Colonists: American Wills and Administrations in the Prerogative Court of Canterbury.* 3 vols. [vol. 1] *1610-1699;* [vol. 2] *1700-1799;* [vol. 3] *1800-1858.* GPC, 1980-81.

————. "Passengers and Ships to America, 1618-1668" (Genealogical Gleanings in England). *National Genealogical Society Quarterly* 71 (1983): 163-92, 284-96; 72 (1984): 132-45.

————. *English Adventurers and Emigrants: Abstracts of Examinations in the High Court of Admiralty with Reference to Colonial America.* 2 vols. [vol. 1] *1609-1660;* [vol. 2] *1661-1773.* GPC, 1984-85.

———. *The Complete Book of Emigrants, 1607-1660: A Comprehensive Listing Compiled from English Public Records of Those Who Took Ship to the Americas for Political, Religious, and Economic Reasons; of Those Who Were Deported for Vagrancy, Roguery, or Non-Conformity; and of Those Who Were Sold to Labour in the New Colonies.* GPC, 1987.

———. *The Complete Book of Emigrants, 1661-1699.* GPC, 1990.

———. *The Complete Book of Emigrants, 1700-1750.* GPC, 1992.

———. *The Complete Book of Emigrants, 1751-1776.* GPC, 1993.

———. *The Complete Book of Emigrants in Bondage, 1614-1775.* GPC, 1988.

———. *Supplement to The Complete Book of Emigrants in Bondage.* GPC, 1992.

———. *The Bristol Registers of Servants Sent to Foreign Plantations, 1654-1686.* GPC, 1988. Supersedes R. Hargreaves-Mawdsley, *Bristol and America . . . 1654-1685.*

———. *Emigrants from England to the American Colonies, 1773-1776.* GPC, 1988. Supersedes Gerald Fothergill, *Emigrants from England, 1773-1776.*

———. *American Wills & Administrations in the Prerogative Court of Canterbury, 1610-1857.* GPC, 1989. Supersedes *English Estates of American Colonists* (q.v.).

———. *Child Apprentices in America from Christ's Hospital, London, 1617-1778.* GPC, 1990.

———. *Emigrants in Chains: A Social History of Forced Emigration to the Americas of Felons, Destitute Children, Political and Religious Non-Conformists, Vagabonds, Beggars and other Undesirables, 1607-1776.* GPC, 1992.

———. *American Wills Proved in London, 1611-1775.* GPC, 1992. This is not a collection of ships' passenger lists, but like one or two other books cited in the Coldham *oeuvre,* it is included to illustrate the full range of Mr. Coldham's contributions.

Coulter, E. Merton, and Albert B. Saye. *A List of the Early Settlers of Georgia.* 1949, 1967. Reprint. GPC, 1983.

Dobson, David. *Directory of Scots Banished to the American Planta-tions, 1650-1775.* GPC, 1983.

————. *Directory of Scottish Settlers in North America, 1625-1825.* 6 vols. GPC, 1984-86.

————. *Directory of Scots in the Carolinas, 1680-1830.* GPC, 1986.

————. *The Original Scots Colonists of Early America, 1612-1783.* GPC, 1989.

————. *Scots on the Chesapeake, 1607-1830.* GPC, 1992.

Faust, Albert B., and Gaius M. Brumbaugh. *Lists of Swiss Emigrants in the Eighteenth Century to the American Colonies.* 2 vols. [vol. 1, Zurich, 1734-44; vol. 2, Bern, 1706-95, Basel, 1734-94]. 1920-25. Reprint (incorporating "Notes on Lists of Swiss Emigrants," 2 vols. in 1). GPC, 1976. See Schelbert.

Filby, P. William. *Passenger and Immigration Lists Bibliography 1538-1900: Being a Guide to Published Lists of Arrivals in the United States and Canada.* 2nd ed. Detroit: Gale Research Company, 1988.

Filby, P. William, with Mary K. Meyer. *Passenger and Immigration Lists Index: A Guide to Published Arrival Records of about 500,000 Passengers Who Came to the United States and Canada in the Seven-teenth, Eighteenth, and Nineteenth Centuries.* 3 vols. Detroit: Gale Research Company, 1981. (Annual *Supplements* published since 1982; *Cumulated Supplements* for 1982-85 (4 vols.) and 1986-90 (3 vols.) have also been published.)

French, Elizabeth. *List of Emigrants to America from Liverpool 1697-1707.* 1913. Reprint. GPC, 1962.

[Galveston]. *Ships Passenger Lists Port of Galveston, Texas 1846-1871.* (Published under the auspices of the Galveston County Gene-alogical Society.) Easley, S.C.: Southern Historical Press, Inc., 1984.

Geue, Chester, and Ethel H. Geue. *A New Land Beckoned: German Immigration to Texas, 1844-1847.* New and enlarged ed. 1972. Reprint. GPC, 1982.

Geue, Ethel Hander. *New Homes in a New Land: German Immigration to Texas, 1847-1861.* 1970. Reprint. GPC, 1982.

Ghirelli, Michael. *A List of Emigrants from England to America 1682-1692*. Baltimore: Magna Carta Book Company, 1968.

Giuseppi, Montague S. *Naturalizations of Foreign Protestants in the American and West Indian Colonies (Pursuant to Statute 13 George II, c. 7)*. Publications of the Huguenot Society of London, vol. 24, 1921. Reprint. GPC, 1964. See Wolfe.

Glazier, Ira A., and Michael Tepper. *The Famine Immigrants: Lists of Irish Immigrants Arriving at the Port of New York, 1846-1851*. 7 vols. GPC, 1983-86.

Glazier, Ira A., and P. William Filby. *Germans to America: Lists of Passengers Arriving at U.S. Ports 1850-[1892]*. 30 vols. to date. Wilmington, Del.: Scholarly Resources, Inc., 1988-(in progress).

————. *Italians to America 1880-1899*. 2 vols. to date. Wilmington, Del.: Scholarly Resources, Inc., 1992-(in progress).

Gonner, Nicholas. *Luxembourgers in the New World*. Dubuque, Iowa, 1889. A "reedition" translated from the German and containing much new material was published in 1987 in two volumes under the editorship of Jean Ensch, Jean-Claude Muller, and Robert E. Owen. (Esch-sur-Alzette, Grand Duchy of Luxembourg: Éditions-Reliures Schortgen.)

Hall, Charles M. *The Antwerp Emigration Index*. Salt Lake City, Utah: Heritage International [1979]. Covers the year 1855 only.

Haury, David A. *Index to Mennonite Immigrants on United States Passenger Lists, 1872-1904*. North Newton, Kan.: Mennonite Library and Archives, 1986.

Hill, Mrs. Georgie A. "Passenger Arrivals at Salem and Beverly, Mass., 1798-1800." *New England Historical and Genealogical Register* 106 (1952): 203-09.

Hocker, Edward W. *Genealogical Data Relating to the German Settlers of Pennsylvania and Adjacent Territory From Advertisements in German Newspapers Published in Philadelphia and Germantown, 1743-1800*. GPC, 1980.

Hotten, John Camden. *The Original Lists of Persons of Quality; Emigrants; Religious Exiles; Political Rebels; Serving Men Sold for a Term of Years; Apprentices; Children Stolen; Maidens Pressed; and Others Who Went from Great Britain to the American Plantations 1600-1700*. 1874. Reprint. GPC, 1974.

Johnson, Amandus. *The Swedish Settlements on the Delaware 1638-1664.* 2 vols. 1911. Reprint. GPC, 1969.

Jones, George F. *The Germans of Colonial Georgia, 1733-1783.* GPC, 1986.

Kaminkow, Jack, and Marion Kaminkow. *A List of Emigrants from England to America 1718-1759.* New ed. Baltimore: Magna Carta Book Company, 1981.

[Kaminkow, Marion.] *Passengers Who Arrived in the United States, September 1821-December 1823.* Baltimore: Magna Carta Book Company, 1969.

Kingsbury, Susan M. *The Records of the Virginia Company of London.* 4 vols. Washington, D.C.: Government Printing Office, 1906-35.

Knittle, Walter A. *Early Eighteenth Century Palatine Emigration.* 1937. Reprint. GPC, 1965. See Tribbeko and Ruperti.

Krebs, Friedrich. "Annotations to Strassburger and Hinke's Pennsylvania German Pioneers." *Pennsylvania Genealogical Magazine* 21 (1960): 235-48.

McDonnell, Frances. *Emigrants from Ireland to America, 1735-1743: A Transcription of the Report of the Irish House of Commons into Enforced Emigration to America.* GPC, 1992.

Mitchell, Brian. *Irish Passenger Lists 1847-1871: Lists of Passengers Sailing from Londonderry to America on Ships of the J. & J. Cooke Line and the McCorkell Line.* GPC, 1988.

————. *Irish Emigration Lists 1833-1839: Lists of Emigrants Extracted from the Ordnance Survey Memoirs for Counties Londonderry and Antrim.* GPC, 1989.

Morton Allan Directory of European Passenger Steamship Arrivals for the Years 1890 to 1930 at the Port of New York and for the Years 1904 to 1926 at the Ports of New York, Philadelphia, Boston and Baltimore. 1931. Reprint. GPC, 1979.

Munroe, J. B. *A List of Alien Passengers, Bonded from January 1, 1847 to January 1, 1851, for the Use of the Overseers of the Poor in the Commonwealth* [Massachusetts]. 1851. Reprint. GPC, 1971.

Myers, Albert Cook. *Quaker Arrivals at Philadelphia 1682-1750; Being a List of Certificates of Removal Received at Philadelphia Monthly Meeting of Friends.* 1902. Reprint. GPC, 1957.

————. "List of Certificates of Removal from Ireland Received at the Monthly Meeting of Friends in Pennsylvania, 1682-1750." In *Immigration of the Irish Quakers into Pennsylvania, 1682-1750*, 277-390. 1902. Reprint. GPC, 1969.

National Archives. *Immigrant and Passenger Arrivals: A Select Catalog of National Archives Microfilm Publications*. 2nd ed. Washington, D.C.: National Archives Trust Fund Board, 1991.

Neible, George W. "Servants and Apprentices Bound and Assigned Before James Hamilton, Mayor of Philadelphia, 1745 [-1746]." *Pennsylvania Magazine of History and Biography* 30 (1906): 348-52, 427-36; 31 (1907): 83-102, 195-206, 351 67, 461-73; 32 (1908): 88-103, 237-49, 351-70.

Nicholson, Cregoe D. P. "Some Early Emigrants to America." *Genealogists' Magazine* 12, nos. 1-16 (1955-58); 13, nos. 1-8 (1959-60). Reprint. GPC, 1965.

Nugent, Nell Marion. *Cavaliers and Pioneers; Abstracts of Virginia Land Patents and Grants [1623-1732]*. 3 vols. Vol. 1: *1623-1666*. Richmond: Dietz Printing Company, 1934 (reprint, GPC, 1963); vol. 2: *1666-1695*. Richmond: Virginia State Library, 1977; vol. 3: *1695-1732*. Richmond: Virginia State Library, 1979.

Olsson, Nils William. *Swedish Passenger Arrivals in New York, 1820-1850*. Chicago: Swedish Pioneer Historical Society, 1967.

————. *Swedish Passenger Arrivals in U.S. Ports 1820-1850 (Except New York)*. Saint Paul, Minn.: North Central Publishing Co., 1979.

Record of Indentures of Individuals Bound Out as Apprentices, Servants, Etc. and of German and Other Redemptioners in the Office of the Mayor of the City of Philadelphia, October 3, 1771 to October 5, 1773. Pennsylvania-German Society Proceedings and Addresses, vol. 16 (1905). Lancaster, Pa.: 1907. Reprint. GPC, 1973.

"Record of Servants and Apprentices Bound and Assigned Before Hon. John Gibson, Mayor of Philadelphia, December 5th, 1772-May 21, 1773." *Pennsylvania Magazine of History and Biography* 33 (1909): 475-91; 34 (1910): 99-121, 213-28.

Revill, Janie. *A Compilation of the Original Lists of Protestant Immigrants to South Carolina, 1763-1773*. 1939. Reprint. GPC, 1968.

Schelbert, Leo. "Notes on Lists of Swiss Emigrants." *National Genealogical Society Quarterly* 60 (1972): 36-46. Additions and corrections to Faust and Brumbaugh.

Schenk, Trudy, Ruth Froelke, and (vol. 1 only) Inge Bork. *The Wuerttemberg Emigration Index.* 6 vols. to date. Salt Lake City: Ancestry, Inc., 1986-. Not mentioned in the text but a useful complement to the Hamburg Emigration Lists.

Schlegel, Donald M. *Passengers from Ireland: Lists of Passengers Arriving at American Ports Between 1811 and 1817.* GPC, 1980.

Schrader-Muggenthaler, Cornelia. *The Alsace Emigration Book.* 2 vols. Apollo, Pa.: Closson Press, 1989-91.

————. *The Baden Emigration Book.* Apollo, Pa.: Closson Press. 1992.

Sheppard, Walter Lee, Jr. *Passengers and Ships Prior to 1684.* Publications of the Welcome Society of Pennsylvania, vol. 1. GPC, 1970.

Skordas, Gust. *The Early Settlers of Maryland: An Index to Names of Immigrants Compiled from Records of Land Patents, 1633-1680, in the Hall of Records, Annapolis, Maryland.* GPC, 1968.

Smith, Leonard H. Jr., and Norma H. Smith. *Nova Scotia Immigrants to 1867.* GPC, 1992.

Stephenson, Jean. *Scotch-Irish Migration to South Carolina, 1772.* Strasburg, Va.: Shenandoah Publishing House, 1971.

Steuart, Bradley W., ed. *Passenger Ships Arriving in New York Harbor. Vol. I (1820-1850).* Bountiful, Utah: Precision Indexing, 1991.

Strassburger, Ralph B. *Pennsylvania German Pioneers: A Publication of the Original Lists of Arrivals in the Port of Philadelphia from 1727 to 1808.* Edited by William J. Hinke. 3 vols. Norristown, Pa.: Pennsylvania German Society, 1934. Reprint. GPC, 1966. (The reprint does not include vol. 2 which contains facsimiles of the signatures to the oaths of allegiance and abjuration, but this has since been reprinted by Picton Press of Camden, Maine and by Genealogical Books in Print of Springfield, Virginia.) See Krebs.

Swierenga, Robert P. *Dutch Immigrants in U.S. Ship Passenger Manifests, 1820-1880: An Alphabetical Listing by Household Heads and Independent Persons.* 2 vols. Wilmington, Del.: Scholarly Resources, Inc., 1983.

Tepper, Michael. *Emigrants to Pennsylvania, 1641-1819: A Consolidation of Ship Passenger Lists from the Pennsylvania Magazine of History and Biography.* GPC, 1975.

————. *Passengers to America: A Consolidation of Ship Passenger Lists from the New England Historical and Genealogical Register.* GPC, 1977.

————. *Immigrants to the Middle Colonies: A Consolidation of Ship Passenger Lists and Associated Data from the New York Genealogical and Biographical Record.* GPC, 1978.

————. *New World Immigrants: A Consolidation of Ship Passenger Lists and Associated Data from Periodical Literature.* 2 vols. GPC, 1979.

————. *Passenger Arrivals at the Port of Baltimore 1820-1834: From Customs Passenger Lists.* Transcribed by Elizabeth P. Bentley, GPC, 1982.

————. *Passenger Arrivals at the Port of Philadelphia 1800-1819: The Philadelphia "Baggage Lists."* Transcribed by Elizabeth P. Bentley. GPC, 1986.

Toups, Neil J. *Mississippi Valley Pioneers.* Lafayette, La.: Neilson Publishing Company [1970]. Additional material is in Bruce Ardoin, "The *Baleine* Brides: A Missing Ship's Roll for Louisiana, 1721." *National Genealogical Society Quarterly* 75 (1987): 303-05.

Tribbeko, John, and George Ruperti. "Lists of Germans from the Palatinate Who Came to England in 1709." *New York Genealogical and Biographical Record* 40 (1909): 49-54, 93-100, 160-67, 241-48; 41 (1910): 10-19. Reprint. GPC, 1965. Includes three Board of Trade lists for 1709 not printed in Knittle.

U.S. Congress. Senate. *Letter from the Secretary of State, with a Transcript of the List of Passengers Who Arrived in the United States from 1st October, 1819, to the 30th September, 1820.* 16th Cong., 2d sess., S. Doc. 118, serial 45. 1821. Reprint. GPC, 1971 (under the title *Passenger Arrivals 1819-1820*).

van Laer, Arnold. J. F. "List of Passengers, 1654 to 1664" (Passengers to New Netherland). In *Year Book of the Holland Society of New York,* 1-28, 1902. Additional material is in Rosalie Fellows Bailey, "Emigrants to New Netherland: Account Book 1654 to 1664." *New York Genealogical and Biographical Record* 94 (1963): 193-200.

Wareing, John. *Emigrants to America: Indentured Servants Recruited in London 1718-1733.* GPC, 1985.

Weslager, C. A. *A Man and His Ship: Peter Minuit and the Kalmar Nyckel.* Wilmington, Del.: Kalmar Nyckel Foundation, 1990.

Whitmore, William H. *Port Arrivals and Immigrants to the City of Boston 1715-1716 and 1762-1769.* GPC, 1973. Excerpted from *A Volume of Records Relating to the Early History of Boston Containing Miscellaneous Papers,* Registry Department of the City of Boston (29th in the series formerly called *Record Commissioners' Reports*), Doc. 100, 229-317. Boston, 1900.

Whyte, Donald. *A Dictionary of Scottish Emigrants to the U.S.A.* Vol. 1. Baltimore: Magna Carta Book Company, 1972.

————. *A Dictionary of Scottish Emigrants to the U.S.A.* Vol. 2. Baltimore: Magna Carta Book Company, 1986.

————. *A Dictionary of Scottish Emigrants to Canada Before Confederation.* Toronto: Ontario Genealogical Society, 1986.

Wolfe, Richard J. "The Colonial Naturalization Act of 1740; With a List of Persons Naturalized in New York Colony, 1740-1769." *New York Genealogical and Biographical Record* 94 (1963): 132-47. Supplements Giuseppi.

Zimmerman, Gary J., and Marion Wolfert. *German Immigrants: Lists of Passengers Bound from Bremen to New York.* 4 vols. [vol. 1] *1847-1854;* [vol. 2] *1855-1862;* [vol. 3] *1863-1867;* [vol. 4] *1868-1871.* GPC, 1985-93.